01

Introduction –
Bosses: the Good, the Bad, and ... Yours

> 66 A good manager is good when people barely know he exists. Not so good when people obey and acclaim him. Worse when they despise him. 99
>
> *Lao-Tzu*

Managers come in as many kinds as there are people. There is no doubt that working for a good one is likely both to make your job easier and to assist you to thrive in your career. You may not be able to choose your manager, but you can certainly influence the way you work with them and they with you. This book is primarily about taking the initiative to create and maintain a good working relationship, one that you will benefit from and enjoy.

Management Characteristics

Managing other people demands a plethora of characteristics, first and foremost of which are those things that enable them to undertake a particular job. In this regard managers may need understanding of and expertise in a host of things to do with industry, product, or technicalities ranging from information technology to fluent French. However, the general characteristics that make someone good at managing others – being a boss – can be listed more definitively. Such characteristics include:

- Having a strategic vision and seeing the broad picture
- Being successful – achieving the results with which they are charged
- Delegating well
- Being decisive (and taking tough decisions as well as routine ones)
- Not procrastinating
- Enthusiasm for the organization, its remit, and its people
- Not playing favorites (indeed treating people as equals)
- Curiosity
- A positive attitude
- Keeping promises
- Providing honest feedback
- Communicating, keeping people informed – and being approachable and listening!
- Being committed to teamwork, involving people, and giving them a chance to contribute
- Embracing change, and considering – and using – new approaches and ideas
- Taking an interest in staff – and actively motivating them
- Having confidence in staff and wanting them to develop (and helping them do so)
- Giving credit for others' success
- Fighting the corner for their team
- Acknowledging their own weaknesses (and mistakes)

Such a list can sound trite, and could certainly be added

to, but if you want to assess either the way your boss stacks up as a boss – or is likely to – then you need to consider such factors. Some characteristics may be more important to you than others (the above is in no particular order); some may be things you want to discuss or plan to work on as you develop a relationship.

On the basis that understanding should precede action, you might also usefully consider two further elements here:

- **What motivates your boss:** if they appreciate good relationships, a sense of order, being in control, a lack of hassle, a challenge, or achieving something new – this and more all make a difference to what they are like to work with. For example, I have worked for bosses whose key motivation was doing new things; inevitably it rubbed off on their staff and made for a stimulating existence. Look too at the negative side of things, asking what your boss dislikes. It may be lack of time, pressure from others, being caught up in details, difficult or emotive decisions; whatever it is, working with them will be easier if you understand and are not unwittingly making a bad situation worse. Some of the flak we take from bosses comes for exactly this sort of reason

- **What management style they use:** most managers work in a way that combines a number of classic styles. They may have a measure of being bureaucratic, consultative, detailed, broad brush, creative, organized, reactive, proactive, or the reverse of these; for example, you may find yourself having to bring order to chaos with a boss who is an organizational disaster (but who may be brilliant in other ways)

! Understanding your boss is the first step to having a good relationship with ● them – and working to create one.

Now, before we concentrate on the positive, let us consider the very worst scenario. Your manager may be an absolute nightmare; certainly the wrong mix of some of the characteristics touched on above can make for some difficulty. Their most constructive comment may be to say things like, *I'm not arguing with you, I'm telling you.* Your most flattering comment about them may be to say, *Their greatest skill is that of intimidation,* and when you get a response from them it may be no more than the ubiquitous Leave it with me followed by silence. More seriously, they may neither appreciate you nor support you, and at worst may resent you and even put you down because they see you as competition.

So, perhaps the first question to ask about your manager is: *Can I work for them?* A poor manager may be a good reason to move on. Realistically, it must be said that there are some people who fall so far below what you hope for in a boss, that all the judicious tactics you can bring to bear will never act to transform them into a paragon of bossly virtue. In those circumstances, the only tactic that does make sense is to move away from them. This is a drastic option, of course; it may mean moving job or employer, and that may not be easy to achieve, certainly not quickly. But there may be no alternative. A period spent in less than ideal circumstances may be acceptable in the short term, especially if you see good prospects ahead. But it is easy to put off a decision to move on, while you constantly think – *Perhaps it will get better*. If a moment's objective thought suggests otherwise, it may be better to bite the bullet rather than delay and just hope fruitlessly.

If that is necessary you need to consider action to relocate, internally or externally, and the details of what is necessary to achieve that are not our concern here. Here we will take a more constructive line and assume that, either in the short term or the long term, you have a boss with whom you *are* able to work. You may feel that the relationship you have could be better, and it is with the process this signals that we are concerned here. What is more, you may have to view a variety of relationships in a similar light. There may be a number of people around your organization with whom you have to work; doing so with the more senior ones can be as difficult as working with an awkward boss. Yet the same principles apply.

> **!** Unless you can influence senior people there is a danger that your job will **●** never be more than reactive; to some meaningful degree you need to be in the driving seat of the relationship.

Overall intentions

It may be true, but it is also a bit vague just to say *I want a good relationship with my boss*. You need to spell out what this means and be clear in your own mind about it. The overall intention here with regard to your working relationship with senior people, and your line manager in particular, is just as it should be for you in your own job. It is to:

- Do those things that get you noticed, taken seriously, and appreciated
- Not do things that make people think less well of you, and therefore rate less highly suggestions you make or initiatives you take, or indeed things you succeed in achieving
- Be able to tackle effectively the individual things that need to be done to gain approval, acceptance, or agreement to what you want for your job (and also for your career)

In this book we consider how you can make your relationships with senior people constructive and useful. Make it your brief to influence a range of senior people in a way that allows you to do your job more effectively and to get more satisfaction from it.

> ! A basic principle is therefore to:
> first impress, then influence.

What is a manager?

Let us be clear. Managers may be concerned with productivity, efficiency, effectiveness, financial measures such as profit or return on sales, and more. To be successful they must deliver, and to do that they must work at the six key areas of managing other people: planning, organizing, recruitment and selection, training and development, motivation, and control.

They may need to work with a variety of different resources to make this possible – but one factor is common: people.

In simple terms the definition of management is: *the achievement of results **through** other people, not for them.* It follows that a manager's greatest asset is therefore their people. Because they cannot do everything themselves, it follows that they stand or fall by the success of their team. As management guru Peter Drucker said, *"The basic task of management is to make people productive."*

> **!** It should never be forgotten therefore
> **●** that it is as much in your manager's
> interest as it is in yours for you to
> work effectively together; that fact is
> the starting point to your success in
> "managing them."

Your greatest asset

Given the role of the manager in an organization and the way people must collaborate and operate together as a team, a good manager can be your greatest asset. Far from being an aggravation or to be avoided (a surprisingly common view of them), they can:

- Help you succeed in your current job
- Develop your competence and skills
- Prepare you for more responsibility
- Help you move on – and up
- Make your working time satisfying, rewarding – even fun

But, as has been said, this does not just happen. The initiative is, at least in part and quite possibly in major part, with you. All you have to do is make sure that they do act to do these things. To make sure of that you need to be clear about what you want from your manager – and equally clear about what they want from you. Let us consider both sides:

1. WHAT YOU WANT FROM YOUR MANAGER

It is important to be clear and practical here (the analysis must set out more than a high salary and a big bonus!). Some relevant factors are obvious:

- Positive ones: being fair, clear in communication, trusting of you, prepared to give responsibility, good at delegating, good at their own job, decisive, consultative, and more
- Negative ones: *not* being secretive, not being prepared to spend time with you, not supportive, and things such as your not wanting them nit-picking at a low level of detail, being dictatorial or resistant to change, and, again, more

You can do worse than actually make your own individual list here. Some factors are of overriding importance. In many surveys, one factor, less obvious than some of those just listed, but one that comes out high in the list of what people want of their bosses, is for them to be: *someone I learn from*. Think about that for a moment. If a job is not to be endlessly repetitive, then this characteristic makes very good sense. It leads to change, creativity, and new challenges that benefit all – you, of course, but also not least the organization for which you and your boss work.

❗ Such factors are akin to objectives. You need to think through what you want **⬤** to promote as an ideal situation, and regard influencing matters in the right direction as an active process.

---

2. WHAT YOUR MANAGER WANTS FROM YOU

No great surprise what tops the list here. The overall answer to this is simple: they want you to do a good job.

You must know – accurately and in some detail – what this means (see also page 21 about job descriptions), and you must appreciate what they think makes it possible.

Ask yourself: How self-starting do they want you to be? How proactive? How creative? What about your time management, productivity, effectiveness, and efficiency? Do they expect you to be good with people and at communication, or to deputize for them on occasion? And what do they *not* want? Certainly they do not want you to be time-consuming to manage or present particular difficulties; especially in any way they regard as being unnecessary or your fault.

Think this through and have a clear view in mind. Not sure? The answer is again simple – *ask them*. Either when you first work with someone, or perhaps following some change, request a chat to sort things out for you both. This is often not done, yet there is surely no reason to avoid such a conversation; it is in the interests of both parties to have things clear. Indeed, it is entirely possible that your initiating such a discussion would be seen as a positive and constructive act; just doing it may score you some points.

> **!** Unless you are clear what you want and
> what is wanted of you, managing senior
> **●** elationships is always going to be akin
> to fumbling in the dark.

The benefits of working effectively together

You need to work with senior people in the right way. That means doing so in a way that they *find* they are content with (rather than just the way that they *think* it should be). Thus it can result as much from your initiative as from their instruction.

The results of getting it right are many and all are worthwhile. When the working relationship is good, your boss and other senior people are more likely to:

- Trust you (and check up on you less)
- Consult, listen to, and give credence to your ideas

- Involve you and delegate to you (and delegate more meaningful tasks and responsibilities)
- Interfere (nit-picking details, for instance) less
- Be reasonable (thinking things through with you, rather than just saying *Do this* and insisting on the first deadline that comes into their mind)
- Support you (in what you do and with other people around the organization)
- Reward you!

You may be able to personalize this list, and add to it – and then you can actively target what you particularly want to occur.

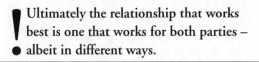

> Ultimately the relationship that works best is one that works for both parties – albeit in different ways.

Testing ways of working

Different people work in different ways. You need to discover what way of working suits you, your boss, and the two of you as a team. Ask by all means, but also experiment. For example, should you:

- Be enthusiastic about them and their plans?
- Praise them (you like being motivated, after all)?
- Be seen to put the job first?
- Involve them in the social life of the office?
- Keep them informed, be their eyes and ears (but not their spy)?

- Aim to share decision making?
- Generate ideas (good, practical ones)?
- Offer opinions openly and often (good, considered ones, that is)?
- Show you can be trusted (to get things done, to keep a confidence)?
- Only ask for help when it is clearly needed (so, for example, not twice with the same problem)?
- Get, or put, agreements and plans in writing?
- Deal with matters at a formal meeting (which you request) or "on the run"?
- Discriminate accurately between what is important and what is less so?
- Take a long-term or short-term view?
- Act as a reminder for them?

The answer in each case, and to other questions you might no doubt add to the list, needs thinking about. While in some cases the answer will surely be yes, in others a particular manager may not like or want it. The detail that follows is important too. For example, consider the question about getting/putting things in writing. There is unlikely to be a blanket answer to this; so, for instance, you need to know not only what areas of things need documenting, but also how this should be done (so that you do not produce a ten-page report when you need a two-page one – or vice versa). When such practice is agreed, stick with it until changes you may think should be made are suggested, discussed, and agreed.

> ❗ Adopt a horses for courses approach
> and balance what you want with what
> ● hey want, and with what is possible.

Corporate culture

Though we have focused so far on individuals – the boss – organizations are important too. They come in all shapes and sizes and the nature of yours will affect the way you act. In one organization, there may be an existing culture that favors good relationships. Time for consultation, consideration of others, and a creative and group approach to things is the norm. In others, the worst kind, secrecy predominates, pressure prohibits consultation, and things are generally more difficult. Your boss works within the culture that exists. If you do not like the way they operate, check out where their behavior originates: you may have not a "difficult" boss, but rather one who is unable to resist following a culture that is essentially unconstructive, at least with regard to the way people work together. This leaves you with three options:

- Work to change the system, making it easier for your boss to work with you (maybe a long and difficult struggle)
- Work with your boss, if not to change the system (though this is an option), then to create an exception (best be open about this and see what the reaction is)
- Work to find a new job (you may conclude that the combination of a difficult boss and an unsympathetic corporate culture is simply incompatible with what

you want in your career). If the culture varies within an organization then the new position may only be down the corridor

It should be said here that various recent developments, ranging from greater competition, more ruthless attitudes within many organizations, to reduced resources (including money and people) have all combined to create a more pressurized workplace. But if you are intent on having a good working relationship with your boss, then leaving things in an unsatisfactory state, especially if all that is done is to hope things will get better, is really not an option.

> ! ● Easy answers cannot be guaranteed in this area. You can, however, adopt a realistic strategy that stands a good chance of paying off in the longer term.

02

The Right Relationship

> ❝I like your qualifications, Gribson – you have the makings of a first-class underling.❞
>
> *Hector Breeze*

Having described managing your boss in terms of creating, maintaining, and working in the right relationship with them, we can now review in more detail how this is defined and achieved.

A Virtuous Circle

Remember that the right working relationship always benefits both parties, and that this fact makes it easier to create what you want – you are not trying to bend your boss to *your* will; rather, you are subtly educating them to recognize that a different way is better to one degree or another for *them*; a way, of course, that also happens to suit you very much.

It is worth working at getting the details of the ideal relationship straight in your mind, getting it agreed, and, over time, keeping it up to date as things change. Bear in mind too that you must not let perfection be the enemy of the good. Realistically you may not ever achieve a perfect relationship, if only because people are not perfect, but you should aim high and get as close as possible to your ideal.

Overall, such a relationship should be:

- **Straightforward**: you should always know how to approach things, for example what needs prior discussion and what can simply be actioned
- **Open and trusting**: time and effort will be wasted if either party is playing games or trying to second-guess the other
- **Linked to clear objectives**: common approaches, with responsibilities, targets, and so on, all known, agreed, and documented where necessary
- **Well defined**: this includes a clear definition of the boundaries between jobs and tasks and responsibilities. It means being clear about rules too (some are necessary and should be respected). By all means campaign to change them (or add to them), but ignoring them or arguing about them causes problems and, worst of all, will mean a manager is less prepared to consult and discuss things that matter more
- **Two-way**: the arrangement should define how both parties operate and interact (not just how you relate to them)
- **Mutually beneficial**: in other words, it must work for both parties, though each may have different agendas and objectives, and realistically some imbalance may occur

! A good relationship – one that works
– encourages more trust and will tend
● to mean your responsibilities increase,
which in turn gives you the opportunity
to show what you can do and thus
increase the trust ... Enough.

Your Job Description

You are never going to be effective and make what you do
impressive if you are not actually completely sure what it
is you are supposed to be doing. Your job description is
not just a formality. Too often these days job descriptions
are regarded as something that is necessary only because
"Human Resources" says so. Employment law has made
them important (for instance, it is difficult to fire someone
for doing an inadequate job if there is no job description
or if it is vague and unclear). That apart, at one level this
should very much be a working tool: one that acts as an aide
memoire between you and your boss. So:

- Make sure that you have one
- Check that you understand it and agree with what it says
- Ask for clarification about anything that is not clear
- Ensure that your boss considers that it reflects real life
  too
- Review it regularly and make sure it stays up to date

The last thing you want if you are to have a good
working relationship with your boss is to have "*I didn't
think that was my job*" type discussions. In terms of progress

and development – getting on and doing more interesting things – the job description provides a foundation from which you can move ahead.

Incidentally, it is often useful to have a look at whatever job description your boss has. They will rarely volunteer it, but you can ask (blame what you have read here). Two things are particularly useful here: firstly, the overall results required, to which you are no doubt required to contribute; and secondly, the boundaries – where your boss's responsibility ends and, by definition, where yours may start. I would go further and suggest that it is worth getting job descriptions of everyone in a department circulated, so that everyone knows not just their individual brief, but also what everyone else is charged with – there is certainly less chance of things dropping between the cracks, as it were, when this is done and everyone is fully informed.

> **Your job description and what it says forms a solid foundation from which to make sure that what you do impresses; make sure it is appropriate.**

A Sound Working Structure

No one can manage anyone well, or for long, on an ad hoc basis. There needs to be a sound basis – a routine and a structure – if the relationship is going to be constructive.

This premise is easy to adopt, but then, unless your boss does all the work and creates exactly what you want, it demands two things:

- **That you think it through.** You need to take the initiative and think about what factors constitute a sound working arrangement. You can do worse than list them
- **That you make it happen.** Again, take the initiative where necessary for creating and agreeing the appropriate basis – and making it stick

Any shortfall here will dilute your efforts to manage others; if you cannot get precisely the arrangement you want first time (and this may well be the case), then you need to keep on working at it.

Amongst the things that help this process are to:
- Adopt a day-to-day routine, especially with regard to how you communicate and how and when you have meetings (see Time Management, on page 26)
- Ensure regular communication (of all sorts, but especially meetings) and ensure you have sufficient time together to agree matters between you
- Make sure that project timing is agreed, and particularly that check points or progress meetings are scheduled in advance (by stage if not by date)
- Agree also the nature and style of all the above: for example, what exactly is a progress meeting? How long is it likely to take, should it be preceded by a written document of some sort, and, if so, what level of detail is involved?
- Make sure that such practice relates appropriately

to tasks (that it is what is needed to get the job done) and to the people (so that all parties feel comfortable with it)

- Address both long- and short-term issues. Think about what is needed day-to-day, right through to annual matters (like planning or appraisal)

It is important to relate all this to the nature of work and tasks. A progress meeting on an essentially routine matter may not take long or involve anything complicated; though it may still be vital to keep things on track. At the other end of the scale, a meeting that is designed to be creative – discussion that aims to identify new ideas or methods – will take longer and is also more likely to be squeezed out by pressure of time on matters that somehow have more immediate urgency. The routine should help make things right along this scale happen effectively.

Describing a good working methodology is one thing, achieving it may well be another. Certainly it will not just happen (unless you have an exceptional manager), or will not happen consistently. So you need to be prepared to think it through, and see it as something else on which you must be prepared to take an initiative. Thus:

- **Ask:** ask, that is, for the opportunity to discuss things, and have some ideas ready (either this can be approached overall, or – better with a less approachable manager – over one issue, a project perhaps, initially as a way of creating good practice)
- **Suggest:** put forward ideas, offer suggestions,

and use what other people (chosen because they will be respected) do to exemplify your case. Discuss, negotiate, request a test (plead?) – but get something agreed, even if it is at first a starting point that you return to and refine to move nearer to the ideal

- **Action:** take the initiative and act assumptively. In other words, just do it. For example, as a project starts, set out a timetable in writing, scheduling progress meetings, and send it without comment, put (or through a secretary get put) the date in the diary, send an agenda ahead of the time and appear ready for the meeting. Taking such action, assuming it is sensible and will be approved, makes sense; your boss may actually find it useful (maybe to the surprise of you both!) and not only react positively but also react well to similar things in future

- **Match their style:** finally, as you approach all this, bear in mind the kind of person they are. What will suit them? Aim high by all means, but if ultimately some compromise is likely to be necessary, plan what you might do. For example, attitude to detail is important here. Your manager may be a "*put it on one page*" kind of person, or want every i dotted, and every t crossed.

You cannot just ignore such characteristics; a well-matched case has the best chance of being agreed – and of working.

> **!●** Start as you mean to go on, suggest something practical, act to get it agreed, and make it work so that they will want it to continue.

Time Management

Time is a resource like any other. And it is an important one; respect for it can boost effectiveness and profitability. Time management can enhance productivity, achieve a focus on priorities, and ultimately act directly to improve your effectiveness. Being a good time manager is definitely a career-enhancing factor and one that can gain you respect with your boss – who is likely to approve, whether it is something they excel at or not.

It is also an area where you and the boss affect each other. You need to agree, early on, a mutually acceptable and useful way of keeping on top of things, and to agree the following:

- How often you meet on a regular basis, when, where, and for how long; this will vary depending on your jobs, but might be once a week (10 a.m. on a Monday to start the week, perhaps)
- How projects are progressed (scheduling meetings to check progress in advance)
- How other contacts are fitted in (do they expect you to come running or respect what else you have on the go?)
- What to do to avoid delay when emergencies hit and you cannot get together

- When and how longer-term issues will be raised (maybe you need monthly or quarterly meetings, again scheduled ahead, to check such issues)

If you are both well organized, then neither will waste the time of the other. So, if good time management is just common sense, why is not everyone a time management expert? Sadly, the bad news is that it is difficult; as the author G. K. Chesterton wrote about

Christianity, declining "not because it has been tried and found wanting, but because it has been found difficult and therefore not tried", so too with time management. There is no magic formula, and circumstances – and interruptions – often seem to conspire to prevent best intentions from materializing. Some people despair, give up, and events manage them.

Few of us organize our time perfectly, but some manifestly cope better than others. Why? Let us take a moment to consider. The key is adopting the right attitude towards the process, seeing it as something to work at, recognizing that the details matter, considering the time implications of everything, and working to get *as close to your ideal time arrangement as possible.*

Little things mount up, and so do small amounts of time saved – you *can* make a difference. The good news is that making consideration of time and its management a habit can work. Bad habits take some effort to shift, but once new ones are established they make the approaches they prompt at least semi-automatic. Thus, while time management takes a conscious effort, establishing good working habits ensures it gets progressively easier.

> **There is an old saying that you should plan the work and work the plan.**

The right principles of so doing are not complex. Three main ones are:

- List the tasks you have to perform
- Assign them priorities
- Do what the plan says

It is the last two that cause problems. Firstly, you cannot do them without understanding what your boss expects of you. Early on in a relationship the allocation of tasks and their priorities must be something they decide or approve. However, it may be useful to *categorize* tasks, for example, grouping telephone calls together. It is certainly useful to plan time for tasks just as you schedule appointments. For example, in conducting presentation skills courses, I find that participants often say they never have enough time to prepare. Yet this is a key task. Skimp preparation time, make a lackluster presentation, and considerable time and work may be destroyed. Putting whatever preparation time is needed in the diary, sticking to that, and avoiding interruptions, must be worthwhile. Yes, this requires discipline – more so if colleagues must get together – but it can be done, and it pays dividends.

It is a fundamental rule of time management to invest some time now to save more time later. Sound preparation of a presentation may take two hours, but how long is involved in replacing a prospect if a sales presentation nosedives? No contest. The same applies to systems; sorting something out so that it works well is time well spent.

How do you stay on plan? The main influences that conspire to keep you from completing planned tasks are: other people and events, and you. Consider these in turn:

First you: you may put off things because you are:

- Unsure what to do
- Dislike the task
- Prefer another task (despite the clear priority)
- Fear the consequences, etc.

Additionally, how much time do you waste by spending *too long* on things because you *like* them? Be honest. Often this is a major cause of wasted time, you flatter yourself that only you can do it so well (even not delegating in case others prove *more able* than you at it?). Such things may be one-off or, worse in their time-wasting potential, regular. Some principles need noting here: like the fallacy that things get easier if delayed. Virtually always the *reverse* is true. For instance, faced with deciding whether to change a system or not, many people will prevaricate. They want to "see how things go," or "check the month-end results" when swift action (necessary and appropriate checking in fact being completed) is best all round.

Next, consider events and other people. One problem

is the classic interruption: the colleagues who, when they say, *Got a minute?* mean that an hour is about to vanish unconstructively. Sometimes saying NO is inherent to good time management. Telephones ringing punctuate our lives (though think carefully about voicemail diluting client service or courtesy). But there are moments to be unavailable; some tasks can *only* be completed in a quiet hour, and take much longer if we are constantly interrupted, especially tasks requiring real thought or creativity.

Good time management gives a real boost to competence. Explore the possibilities, instigate good habits and avoid any dilution of your firm intentions, and the results might surprise you.

This is very much an area where boss and employee must work together. For example, your boss may need to understand that it is best not to interrupt you while you finish writing a report (because it will be done better and quicker). You need to accept that your boss has priorities of their own, that they are not always available, and you need to plan your own time and work accordingly.

! ● Mutually agreed, and better still similar, methods of organizing time and viewing productivity are a sound fundamental basis for a good working relationship between boss and employee.

The Social Dimension

All that has been said so far assumes a very businesslike situation. So it will be – in part. But the workplace is also a social environment. Whatever the pressure for productivity, people interact at a social level: they chat, they have a drink after work, and, especially in open-plan offices, people have a plethora of informal contacts as work progresses. Work would be a real drudge without this. But that does not mean such interactions must be entirely haphazard or overdone! You need to decide to what extent to befriend your boss. If you can create a good informal relationship alongside the more formal one, it will make things less stressful and help oil the wheels of the whole relationship.

The trick is to find a level of interaction in this respect that suits you, and your boss (who should see it as appropriate and not read it as toadying for favors), and which does not alienate others – colleagues – in the process. It will clearly cause difficulties if anyone, certainly anyone significant, thinks that you are sucking up to the boss and creating a relationship that is to their disadvantage.

So, consciously engage in some contact that meets these criteria, for example:

- **Share small talk**: keep off contentious issues with your boss (the dire state of your relationship with your partner or, conversely, the ecstasy of the night before, perhaps); maybe you should also draw in colleagues to some of these discussions expressly so that they do not feel you are overpowering them
- **Respect your boss's situation**: they may be under

pressure, they may appreciate your beating a deadline and everyone may like it if you have done so by collaborating with a colleague and say so: the colleague feels included and respected and your boss likes the idea of the team working well together

- **Be appreciative**: if you like what you are doing, some special project you have been involved in or anything else, why not say so; courtesy costs nothing, as they say. Regular thanks can also be a way of reinforcing knowledge about your likes and dislikes and can help steer your involvement in the right direction

- **Remember**: take on board what is going on in your boss's life. It is nice to remember significant moments – an evening out, kids' exams, their birthday (maybe it could be you that organizes colleagues to mark suitable occasions in some way). Doing this might even encourage them to remember more about your own important events

If this all seems a bit contrived, so be it. It is better to act in a considered manner than find there is a whole area of your relationship that you are allowing to be peppered with inappropriate gaffs. One or two may not matter, but a regular string of them may change the atmosphere between you.

One last comment, which is preceded by firmly saying that further details go beyond our brief here. Be careful of any romantic involvement with your boss. I have no wish to be a killjoy, I know such things can sometimes work – but more commonly they end in tears (so much so that many larger organizations have firm policies about the clash of interests that can be involved here). Be grateful if this does not arise – and be warned.

That said, and flagged as something that may well give you the wrong image with a whole range of people, we will move on in the next chapter to examine how you can create a positive image and how this helps the whole process of dealing with – and managing – senior people.

03

Establishing a Positive Profile

66 Nothing succeeds like reputation. 99
John Huston

How you will be able to work with your boss and whether working together will be a constructive relationship is not only influenced by what you do, it is also influenced – for good or ill – by how you are seen. In some senses this may be unfair. But the world – and the world of work too – is apt to be unfair and this must be taken as read.

Perception Is Reality

How you come over to other people matters, and your boss is no exception. It was Oscar Wilde who said, *Only shallow people do not judge by appearances*, and you would be wise to take note of the principle implied in this.

Are you a force to be reckoned with? If you say *I think we should do X*, do your manager and other senior people listen and take on board what you have to say? Or do they just say to themselves, What would they know?, make nice noises but actually take little or no notice? If you are to be a power in the land as it were, you do need to be positive about yourself – and you need to cultivate a "professional" exterior image too.

That sounds fine. We all like to think we are professional. But what exactly does "being professional" mean? It is, like beauty, largely in the eye of the beholder. If you are to appear professional in the eyes of your boss, you need to think about what that means to *them*. How do your own manager and others view, rate, and judge other people? You need to think about this and adapt accordingly.

! **If you hesitate to spend some time and thought on this area, thinking perhaps** ● **that it is unnecessary and that your good work alone should be sufficient to categorize you as a key player, remember this old maxim – if you look like a doormat, then in all likelihood people will walk all over you.**

It is worthwhile to assess the impression you give and, if necessary, work on enhancing it.

Key Objectives

There is one particular reason to worry about your profile. Your power to influence is directly affected by how you are seen, and how well you influence affects much else. Your manner, appearance, way of working, and how you conduct yourself all contribute to how you are seen.

You therefore have some key objectives, including being seen as:

- Competent
- Confident
- Credible

Other factors are important too – being seen as "professional" may mean you need to be seen as experienced, knowledgable, expert, creative, thorough, one who gives attention to detail, is honest (about everything from opinions to deadlines), up to date, reliable, well-organized, and has qualities ranging from being a good listener to having empathy for other people – but perhaps those three highlighted above are especially important for influencing a boss. You need to decide just how to interpret every such characteristic given your own situation. You may have such qualities in abundance (of course you do!), but are they sufficiently apparent?

For example, you may be a well-organized person, there is nothing essentially wrong with your productivity, and you do your work well. However, if your desk always looks as if it has been hit by a tornado, or if you are always the last to arrive at meetings, and do so clutching an untidy heap of files and papers, then at the very least this will dilute the extent to which others see you as well organized. Adjusting this situation will boost one aspect of your profile. If there is a series of areas needing this kind of attention, then if you address each of them in a similar way, each will contribute more to the overall impression that you want to give. It makes sense and it may prove surprisingly easy to make adjustments that have this kind of effect.

The Right Image

What is being said here is that this is something you should spell out to yourself. What qualities must be in evidence before *you* are seen as "professional"? You can probably add to the list above, certainly you should personalize it; and maybe prioritize it too, so that you focus on those characteristics that are most important in *your* particular job and with your boss, rather than those making up some general list. Keep the organizational culture in mind as you consider this. This may dictate that factors such as being respectful or ethical are important. To take a simple example, consider dress codes. You may work in an environment where a range of formality is acceptable; but you still need to decide where on such a scale you feel you should be seen to be.

You should be clear what is right for you and, to make analysis more manageable, it may help to see your list grouped into three categories:

- **Your inherent qualities**: those that shine through and need no great attention (they may be an ongoing part of your work and always in evidence)
- **Qualities that do need acquiring or could use some strengthening** (for example, if being a good communicator is important, maybe a useful first step might be to improve your report-writing style)
- **Qualities that can benefit from some *exaggeration***

This last – exaggeration – is a valid technique, but should not be overdone. In some professions extreme exaggeration

is endemic; for instance, many an actor has rued the day
they listed an ability to ride a horse or motorcycle on their
resumé, and has the bruises to remind them.

> **!** **Making people aware of how you
> operate and what you have to offer is
> ● an active process.**

Three additional points may be useful:

- Firstly, one caveat: do not overdo things here. You
  do not want a reputation for being unpleasantly
  "*pushy*". But this is not what is meant here. For
  example, you might decide that being seen as
  someone who gives attention to detail is important
  (maybe with certain people or projects). The way
  to do this, or anything else for that matter, is not
  to say so, it is to *show* it. If this goes beyond your
  natural tendencies then you may need to enhance
  the ability and exaggerate it somewhat

- Secondly, you might also list and work on
  characteristics that you should avoid and *be
  seen not to embrace*. For example, few managers
  appreciate time-wasters, whingers or people who
  spend half their office life engaged in office politics
  or conducting private business on the internet

- Lastly, explaining what you are doing may avoid
  negative impressions or enhance positive ones. For
  example, you might be noted as, *Wasting time on
  the internet* or you might explain that you are using

your lunchtime to do some research (valid research, that is; the internet contains many unsuitable distractions – some of which have cost people their jobs)

Who To Impress

Having worked out what qualities you need to have in evidence and how to make them appropriately visible, you need to think about to whom you direct this impression. Being clear about who actually constitutes your "target group" will ensure no one is missed and no time is wasted. Think about it. Make a list. It will probably include:

- Your immediate supervisor or manager
- Their immediate manager
- Other senior people with whom you work (in other departments or functions, perhaps)
- Senior people with whom your employment involves you (adding people like HR managers and trainers)
- "Gatekeepers": a group consisting of those who prevent or allow easy access to others (such as a secretary or assistant)
- "Communicators": a group who can communicate news or opinion about you (these may range from the office gossip to whoever runs an internal newsletter)
- External contacts: for instance, if you deal with customers

Some care is necessary here. It is easy to overlook the influence of someone you perhaps see as peripheral.

Someone's secretary, for instance, may have a minor role in your life, but the fact that they are a trusted aide to their own boss may mean that their opinion of you may count for quite a lot. Some people here may interact with you a good deal already. Others may be worth forging stronger links with. Many of these sorts of people are in a position to influence how your boss will work with you because your boss's opinion of you comes, in part, from information and impressions given by these people.

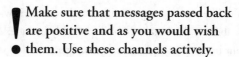

Make sure that messages passed back are positive and as you would wish them. Use these channels actively.

It is important not to be caught up on this area as something that becomes a time-consuming preoccupation and a distraction from your real work. The vast majority of things that can be done to enhance your image come through your work – doing it well, or adding little touches to make your position clear. So, many of the points made as this text continues can usefully be linked back to this principle (and we revisit the principle in the *Afterword*). Of course, if you can think of anything of major significance in your own job that adds weight here, then it is worth taking advantage of it. I can well remember, when my first book was published, how it suddenly helped others to see me in a different light.

This personal example makes a further point. The things that will act in this way for you are linked to the culture in which you work. They may be linked to:

- The technical nature of your field of work
- The size, location or history of the organization for which you work
- Any international dimension to your organization or work

The possible range is considerable, but here is another example I have come across that is linked to languages. Someone speaking fluent French, and using this on an occasional basis in their work, is adding to their corporate persona. If, in due course, they wish to be relocated overseas, this may well help their chances of achieving this. In the case I am thinking of, this has indeed happened, the person concerned being posted first to America and then to China – in neither case have they actually used their French, but the next stop looks like being Geneva.

To return to Oscar Wilde, people really do put a great deal of weight on how people appear – not least sometimes making snap judgments that color their view for some time. (Snap judgments can produce sound judgment. As I write, Malcolm Gladwell's book Blink is being acclaimed for its review of this phenomenon, and it is well worth a look.) Influencing this as much as possible, and having a clear idea of how, ideally, you want to be thought of, is a sound basis for better interaction with your boss and others.

66 I don't want yes-men around me.
I want everybody to tell me the truth,
even if it costs them their job. 99

Samuel Goldwyn

This famous quotation implies that bosses just want people to do as they are told. To some extent this is true, but they want more, often including a degree of self-sufficiency and they judge how well they can work with someone not least by how they appear.

04

Working to Create Impact

66 Anyone can do any amount of work, provided it isn't the work he is supposed to be doing at the moment. 99

Robert Benchley

Without devaluing what has been said in the last chapter, there are some further, very tangible, factors that contribute to the success of your working relationships with senior people. All relate to the job you do and to being – and being seen to be – effective. In one organization where I worked certain people were described as being "good operators." The importance of being so was demonstrated by the fact that there was a special internal phrase for it.

Ready, Aim, Fire!

To establish and maintain a good working relationship with your manager you have to be seen as effective, so you must actually be effective – and to be effective you need to aim at the right things. It means having the right targets in mind. This, in turn, means:

- Being clear about your aims and responsibilities (the comments about job descriptions earlier are relevant here)
- Understanding – and hitting – all those specific targets that may be part of your remit (never underestimate

the importance of this, or how much failing to do so may affect you in the boss's eyes)

- Delivering (with a capital D) – doing what is expected of you (and doing more than is expected has even more impact)
- Your performance being trouble free, and being noticed (and here it may be that your boss should be aware not only that you have succeeded, but of the details: that something was on time despite unexpected problems, that you carried other people with you, and so on)

It is an old adage, but true:

> **!** Never confuse activity with achievement. No manager will be impressed, or easier to deal with, just because they know you are "busy". It is results that matter, not least because your results reflect on your manager – they get credit from having a successful team.

What You Do And How You Do It

The workplace is hectic. It is pressurized and many people, including bosses, spend much of their time dealing with the unexpected. It should not be surprising in such an environment if sometimes managers seem to notice *nothing*. Ultimately, however, achieving goals does have a positive impact.

So too do the ways in which you work; for example, it normally pays to:

- Be thorough, with all the details accommodated and no loose ends left outstanding
- Be consistent and reliable, so that you get a reputation for "delivering" (this alone can put you at the front of the queue when interesting, and important, projects are allocated, just as perceived gaps in your competence can lead to you not being involved in what you want)
- Match with your manager, reflecting their requirements and concerns while adding in your own
- Have the right attitude. It is probably best to be interested, maybe even enthusiastic, about most things. However, you do not want to become a dumping ground for unwanted work – *Patrick never complains* – so a balance here is necessary

But whatever else, enthusiasm is infectious (and those described as *fired with enthusiasm* might just be so called because they did *not* exhibit it).

Delivering – The Essentials

Almost whatever job you do, and at whatever level, three things are of overriding importance if your work is to be effective and to impress. These are that it should be:

- **On spec:** having a clear brief has been mentioned – the first thing to deliver is *exactly what was agreed* *or asked for.* If there is difference it should only be a positive one (but even that might collect a reprimand if other things were more important; perfectionism is not an automatic virtue in respect of every possible task)

- **On time:** ensure you meet any deadline (provided it is agreed and possible; and never be railroaded into agreeing impossible deadlines – the only response to your saying, *I told you there was insufficient time* will be to be told, *Then you shouldn't have agreed the date.* Yes, in a sense this is unreasonable, but this attitude has some logic and certainly it reflects real life – rarely will people say *I should have given it more thought*)

- **On budget:** money matters more than many things in organizational life. Try not to get into a position where agreed budgets are exceeded (or planned cost reductions missed). Creating pleasant surprises – saving significant money, for instance – in this area will be noticed, and welcomed, but beware of setting precedents

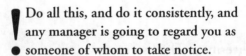

> ! ● Do all this, and do it consistently, and any manager is going to regard you as someone of whom to take notice.

Delivering – Creating A Balance

Linking to the previous comments, it is worth bearing in mind a juggling act that applies to many things. Imagine, in the diagram shown on page 47, that the lines are elastic.

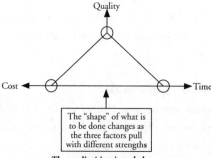

The quality/time/cost balance

The blend of the three elements – quality, time, and cost – may always be a compromise; for example, spend less and quality may be reduced (as it says in one American management book – *they didn't want it right, they wanted it Wednesday*). Get the balance right – something else to ask about and agree perhaps – and the outcome of what you do will be more secure. The diagram here is a very easy thing to keep in mind: when you make adjustments to one of these factors bear in mind the effect this adjustment has on the others. As an example, consider the judgments to be made about writing and producing this book. If it is too short it may appear insubstantial, but it will be less expensive to produce and quicker to read. If it is longer, it may contain more information, but it will cost more to produce, and thus a higher price will be set for it, and it will take longer to read. The various elements are interrelated. Change one, and others automatically change as well. The result of this kind of deliberation about anything is usually a compromise; in the case of this book we intend it to be a good one – sufficient ideas and information, yet an affordable item that does not take an unacceptable amount of time to read and consider (tell me if you have a useful view!).

Doing Your Homework

Success needs setting up. In other words, if you charge in unthinkingly and then fail, then you may well conclude that you have only yourself to blame.

Thus, it makes sense to always:

- **Do the necessary groundwork**. Check facts and figures, consider the details, and do any research that puts you in a position to complete the task satisfactorily
- **Ask others where necessary**. Do this informally as much as in any other way – a good networking system helps everyone. Certainly never try to proceed with something with one hand tied behind your back for want of the answer to a simple question
- **Ask your manager for any necessary support**. If they must be involved at some stage, arrange how and when this will be, or, if they need to give permission for you to access files or set up discussions with people who are *their* colleagues, get that organized. It is always better to say something early on, rather than admit you need support halfway through, maybe with things not going well, especially if it then puts your manager under pressure to provide support at short notice when they have other priorities

Experience changes things. Fail to ask for support or

talk to the right person and the project may fail. Do it and not only is the project successful, but next time you will be that much more self-sufficient.

! **Running before you can walk or with the wrong shoes can only trip you up.**
● **Organize yourself to be successful.**

A Good Idea!

Managers are not paid to have all the good ideas that keep their department (company or whatever) running successfully. It is possible that, if they were, not many would succeed. Rather they are paid to *make sure there are enough good ideas to do just that*. Where do all these ideas come from? A sensible manager will regard the best source of ideas as their people who – separately or together (two heads are better than one) – can contribute what is necessary.

Good bosses get this to work better than bad bosses, because it works best when there is a good relationship, people are well motivated, and *want* to contribute. The fact that staff are often much closer to some of the areas of work in need of ideas can help too.

Not everyone can contribute equally in this way, of course. The jobs people do and the knowledge and experience they build up may put them in a position where this is difficult; or some may simply not be "ideas people" (though they have other strengths that benefit the team). But if you are one of those who does contribute – indeed if you can become one of those who can be relied upon

not only to contribute when asked, but to take a lead –
this can only help to position you in a way that will make
achieving other things easier. It is a factor that can affect
your relationship with a boss very positively. So if you
think you can contribute in this way (surely you can!) then
you need to be able to organize so that you can do so. For
instance:

- Think through any embryo suggestion thoroughly
  (to the extent of doing any research or checking
  that may be needed)
- Suggest it, and suggest it in the best possible way.
  Will a chance remark do? Should you introduce it
  during a meeting (where others may lay claim to
  it)? Does it need a written note?
- Be prepared for rejection. However creative
  you are, not every idea will be right or possible
  to implement. There may be many reasons for
  this; for example, an idea may well be rendered
  inappropriate because of facts outside your
  knowledge, so you need to accept that a proportion
  of ideas will inevitably be rejected. But the only
  way to get some ideas accepted is to stick your neck
  out and try, learn from the experience, and your
  strike rate will increase

An example makes an additional point. I once met
someone struggling in a new job. They complained that
their boss had brought them in to shake up and develop
an existing small department, yet they said, *Every idea I*

suggest seems to be rejected. I looked at some of the memos setting out ideas and improvements; they seemed sound. But the language was powerful: existing procedures were castigated as better ways of doing things were suggested. I asked who had set up the existing way of working, and it did not surprise me to learn that it was the boss. In effect what was happening was that each suggestion was saying, *Your way is inadequate/bad, here is the right way of doing it.* Not surprisingly, this was making the boss defensive. Resubmitting the plans in a way that positioned everything in a different way – *this has worked well and is a necessary system, but given the increase in volumes* (i.e. reference to something that had changed) *in future this can be made to work even better* – apparently magically started to prompt agreement.

This example seems obvious with hindsight, but it is exactly this kind of thing that makes a difference. It stresses the value of objective consideration of any problem. Good ideas presented with enthusiasm were failing to be accepted just because of the history involved; always take account of the broad picture and of people's feelings – especially the boss's.

You need to have confidence in your ideas, as another example shows. Any pharmaceutical product is necessarily subject to many tests before it can be marketed to the public (a complex process that in most countries is regulated by government). The last stage consists of clinical trials; that is, doctors use the product with a limited number of patients and report back to the producer.

In one company they were launching a new product, a gel to treat mouth ulcers, and had reached the stage of such clinical trials. Information was slow to come in and the marketing manager became concerned about the effect on the subsequent schedules and launch date. His secretary, aware of this, thought about it and had an idea. It seemed so obvious that, for a while, not wishing to appear stupid by perhaps suggesting something that had been thought of and rejected for good reason, she said nothing. But as the delay became worse she plucked up courage. *Surely, she said, the people who would hear about patients with mouth ulcers are not doctors, they're dentists.* Eureka! Obvious or not, they had not thought of it (all previous products had clearly been for prescription by doctors). The test was restarted with a panel of dentists and, in due course, the launch proceeded on time.

Moral: many aspects of the organization you work for need ideas, and most bosses do not care who has them, they are just grateful for them when they come. In the kind of circumstances described above, the worst that could have happened would be for the idea to be inappropriate; while it could not then have been used, the interest taken would no doubt have been applauded. The situation is always wide open, and the next idea you contribute might be the one that matters. It certainly might add to your positive profile.

> ❗ The only way to get a nil rejection rate
> is never to put forward ideas; and this
> ● is *not* the way forward. In most jobs an
> element of creativity is essential to success.

Enhancing The Impact Of What You Do

Beyond delivering (with a capital D), in addition you should:

- Undertake some internal public relations – albeit judiciously – to tell people that you are effective (this might range from simply copying additional people with something, to volunteering to write something for the company newsletter or make a presentation about a project with which you have – successfully – been involved)

- Associate yourself with success (for example, associate with successful people, perhaps some more senior ones and certainly not with the office gossip or troublemaker)

- Use success to secure new challenges, not just asking to be involved but quoting other experiences – *Now that I have done Y ... an involvement with X surely makes sense*

- Be generous to work colleagues: claiming *all* the credit when others manifestly contributed is rarely acceptable

> ❗ The combined effects of such
> strategies may improve your standing
> ● sufficiently for you to achieve more of
> what you want.

Certainly you should recognize the importance of this aspect of your profile. It is an inherent factor in how your boss sees you, and thus how they treat you and work with you. It follows that you must see this kind of activity as an ongoing dimension of your work life. Your focus – and time spent – on it must be kept in proportion; no one is suggesting that you make personal publicity a full-time activity, but you should look at every aspect of your work with an eye on this area and continuously watch for opportunities to create and maintain the positive profile that you decide that you need. Remember that being effective and generating the right results remains paramount; perception rarely makes up for actual deficiencies in performance, though it can certainly enhance performance and help create a better overall feeling about your work.

The next thing to consider, an inherent part of any working relationship, is communications. It is to this we turn in the next chapter.

05

Communicating with Senior People

66 One should not aim at being possible to understand, but at being impossible to misunderstand. 99

Marcus Fabius Quintilian

Communications of all sorts around an organization are important. Communications are literally the driving force of the organization; almost to the extent that it is true to say that if there were no communications, there would be no action, activity, or success.

Perhaps because the task of getting a communication right is too often underestimated – an assumption being made that it is a straightforward process and little care or consideration being taken over it – the resulting poor communications can cause problems. We see evidence of this all around us; I saw a notice on the back of a hotel bedroom door that said: "*In the interests of security, please ensure that your bedroom door is securely closed before entering or leaving the room.*" A good trick if you can do it. Not only did someone write this, they had it printed and affixed to more than 200 doors and still did not notice it was nonsense. Breakdowns in communications are all too common: listen carefully in most organizations and you will overhear the results – *But I thought you said ... That's not what I meant.* Often no great harm is done (though it may cause annoyance), but sometimes it is; time or money is wasted, a deal is lost, or an ill-considered comment in a report comes back to haunt someone months, even years, after it was written.

So, care is needed in communicating – and dealing with your boss or other senior people may only compound the problem.

Barriers To Communication

When your boss misunderstands you it is annoying and can cause problems. But rather than just saying, *What's the matter, don't they understand anything?*, check whether it might perhaps be your fault. There are a number of inherent problems that make achieving clear communication difficult; if you understand this, and use specific techniques toovercome them, you will have fewer problems – and, apart from avoiding misunderstandings, being seen as a good communicator is likely to stand you in good stead with your boss and others.

The problem is that people generally do not listen, find it difficult to understand, are reluctant to agree or act, and make things more difficult by providing inaccurate or inadequate feedback; and senior people are no exception. Consider these problems in turn:

- **Paying attention:** Everyone, especially a busy boss, finds it difficult to listen (or to concentrate on reading), certainly for a long time. Long monologues are resented, so even something like this book is designed to fall into many sections and uses many headings to provide breaks and stop it being seen as difficult to access. In addition, people are selective; they pay attention to what seems to *them* to be important and may make the wrong assumptions about what are, in fact, the key parts of a message

The moral: you have to work hard at making sure your message really is taken in

- **Understanding:** There are a number of natural human reactions that act to dilute understanding. People always make assumptions based on their past experience – *sounds a bit like ... to me.* If you do not take that into account there can be no frame of reference to which your message can link. Jargon can be a problem. It may provide a convenient shorthand between people in the know, but can confuse others. Further, people are reluctant to say that they do not understand something in case this makes them look stupid; and few bosses want to look stupid in front of their staff, so perhaps less checking than is useful goes with the territory. Assumptions are often made before someone even finishes what they are saying, as someone says to themselves – *I know where this is going.* At that point their mind stops concentrating on listening and most of their mental energy goes on planning a response. Things spoken but not seen may be more easily misunderstood. Thus showing things may be useful, so too is a message that "paints a picture"

The moral: expect achieving understanding to need care

- **Agreeing:** This takes us further towards persuasion (the subject of a later chapter). People are often suspicious of those with "something to sell." If agreeing to something might leave them open to being shown to be wrong, and thus involves an element of risk, that too can push people away from coming to an agreement

The moral: even a strong case, which logic dictates should be accepted, may still be resisted

- **Taking action:** Taking action may mean someone has to change a habit (perhaps of a lifetime!), action also gets people considering the risk – *if I do this and it doesn't work out, what then?* – and some people simply find decision making hard and will sit on the brink of it forever if they can. Certainly bosses are not immune to this, and if too often their indecisiveness is final then it can be very frustrating

The moral: even when the argument seems to have been accepted and there is no logical reason not to act, recognize that more may need to be done in order to prompt that action

- **Obtaining feedback:** People are not always open in communication. They may hide their feelings, intentionally or for other reasons (perhaps from embarrassment or uncertainty), or what they do offer by way of feedback may be difficult to interpret, so, *Fine* may actually mean, *I am too busy to take that in, but it doesn't seem very important anyway*

The moral: feedback often needs to be teased out, and it must never be forgotten that appearances can be deceptive. In the hectic modern workplace, time pressure certainly accentuates this problem

All this begins to explain some of the difficulties that communication regularly produces. It may even persuade you that your boss is normal rather than being difficult! The first task here is simply to recognize and remember the likely problems. If you *expect* difficulties in these kinds of ways – and you should – then that is the first step to getting over them. There is help at hand, however, because other inherent factors about the nature of communication can act to assist in getting your messages across successfully; again, the trick is to know what these things are, and to use them appropriately.

Aids To Understanding

The four factors below (stemming from what psychologists call the "laws of learning") all provide assistance to the process of making communications successful. They can be described as:

- **Addressing the individual's questions:** What is people's first response to any message? They think about its affect on them. They want to know if it will affect them, and if so whether the effects will be positive or negative. They may well not voice this, but they do think it; it is an instinctive reflex. This is surely easy enough to understand; it is what we all do ourselves. Knowing this, we can include something about any effects that what we say will have on our boss within a message, addressing the problem rather than leaving a host of questions floating in the air. This may often be as simple as the difference between saying – *do this and productivity will be improved* – and saying something like – *do this and your workload will be easier to cope with, you will have more time to concentrate on priorities and productivity will increase*. Remember: every time you ask your boss for something, they do not just consider what it means for you, or even for the business, but also what it means for them; indeed the latter may come first

- **Making it logical:** This is no more than choosing to go through things in a logical order (and perhaps explaining what that order is). Information is better retained in the order in which it is taken in. If we have to re-sort it, something may be lost in the process. Consider something like your telephone number. You know it backward. Well, do you? You certainly know it forward, but trying to recite it backward demonstrates the different thinking process involved and probably takes a moment longer. So, give people things in the right order so that no sorting is necessary, and they can consider and use the information more easily. If your message comes over in random bits – *and another thing* – it will never be as powerful. This is an especially good way to enhance the attention your boss gives you. If they know that you reliably put things in a clear, logical way then you will find you have their ear more easily than those who do not. As this is not the most common characteristic, it also impresses

- **Linking to experience:** Whatever anyone says to anyone else is considered in the light of their prior experience. For instance, if your boss asks for some figures, consider what goes through their mind if you say – *I'll need to check with the computer.* Perhaps this creates a vision of instant efficiency and good service; but perhaps not. It depends on what prior experiences with computer systems come to mind. The same kind of response always happens. If you link accurately to your boss's experience, understanding is easier; if you misjudge what they know already, or assume they have experiences that in fact they have not, confusion can result. Specific linking – *this will be like the meeting we had to discuss increasing sales* – with your boss, summoning up an image a constructive two-hour meeting that really got some new ideas on the go, makes what follows that much easier

- **Repeating:** Any message, especially a complex one, may be better taken in if it is repeated. Any message, especially a complex one ... no, that does not mean simply repeating the same words again and again. It means that finding acceptable ways to repeat key parts of a message can be useful in reinforcing understanding. Considering a number of examples makes this clear (and adding an example is itself just a way of introducing repetition). A meeting followed by the issue of minutes of the proceedings is repetition. Something said and demonstrated, or illustrated by a visual aid, is repetition. So is something that summarizes. Or checked – *that's important, let me put it another way*. You can probably think of more examples, and are conscious of doing this in various ways already. Deploying repetition as an intentional technique can strengthen understanding and avoid unnecessary misunderstanding.

The message here is simple, but it has a plethora of implications. Communications can be inherently difficult. Your boss is probably no more subject to the inherent problems than anyone else (well, maybe a little!).

You will communicate more easily and more accurately if you understand what difficulties are most likely to arise, and why, and if you utilize other inherent aspects of the communications process to help overcome these difficulties and assist in getting your message over accurately and smoothly.

The Basic Principles

Fact: organizations have hierarchies and these do mean something. The overall trend may be towards flatter organization structures and more informal styles, but senior people are, well, senior. There is therefore something of a balancing act to be performed in relating to such people, and you need to:

- Cultivate friendly relationships
- Maintain an appropriate degree of respect and distance
- Create a good *working* relationship with people (almost every aspect of this book comes back to this)

Do not be put off by bad communication on the part of others (and, yes, senior people can be as guilty of this as anyone else). Get things clear and, if they are not, ask; and watch for remarks that can, wittingly or otherwise, skew your response: like the boss who says, *I think this is a great idea, what do you think?* Is this a request to agree, or do they really want your objective opinion?

 Balance respect for and involvement with others to create appropriate positioning on the hierarchical ladder.

The Right Time

Assuming that you are relating to people in the right sort of way, another important factor is timing. Consider two possibilities:

1. THEY COMMUNICATE WITH YOU

One philosophy follows the old adage that if a senior person says *Jump!* then the only response is to ask *How high?* But is this always right and do senior people always expect it? There are certainly occasions when the right reaction to a "summons" is to stall. You may want to finish something more important (or let them decide which is most important) or to have time to prepare for whatever the discussion will be about. So, be prepared to stand up for yourself. Be polite but be prepared to be firm (you may not always succeed, but you may achieve a surprisingly good rate of strike). Busy bosses can be abrupt and inconsiderate. Your phone rings and they say, *Pop in for a minute, will you?* Before you say that you will rush off to their office, consider other responses, for example:

- Can you find out what it is about? (Just ask)
- Having done so, is this a good moment for you, or would you value being able to collect your thoughts? (Consider)
- Can you make an alternative suggestion? (*Could we deal with this when we meet as planned tomorrow? Do you want to do this, ahead of me finishing that?*)

Sometimes, of course, circumstances do not allow this or the response is simply that only now will do. But there is some merit in being seen not just to drop everything every time, not least since it shows that you have a mind of your own. One proviso: don't just moan – *it's a bad time for me* – but respond in a way that focuses on work and suggests suitability for both parties.

2. YOU COMMUNICATE WITH THEM
In which case the rule is clear: Always choose your moment – and do so carefully.

Again there is a balance to be struck. Insist too much – *But I must see you today!* – and, if they agree, you may find that you have given yourself a very difficult meeting (time is short and their mind is on other things). Leave things too long and the moment passes, the project has run on too long or, perhaps worst of all, the problem has got worse. In the latter case you are on a hiding to nothing, and saying *But I've been trying to get to see you for days* only makes matters worse – *If you'd told me what it was about, you would have been able to see me earlier.*

A Good Moment

Conversely, when you have someone's full attention, when they feel the meeting (or, indeed, any other form of communication) is necessary, appropriately set up, and likely to fit in with the many other things they are probably doing – then you are more likely to get a good hearing.

But – be realistic. Offices are busy places. You might want an hour with someone, but is this likely to be agreed, and, if it is, will it be resented? Compromise if necessary, but you have to try to make the compromise work.

So:

- **Consider timing carefully.** Even in small ways timing always needs thinking about. Do you interrupt that meeting, stop them on their way out of the office, or set a special session?
- **Plan, and schedule, ahead as far as possible.** And work out a mutually acceptable way of dealing with matters that are urgent or unexpected

- **Stick to time.** Always be on time for meetings. Always set a start and finish time for meetings you set or request. And give reasonable notice whenever possible. Some things are inevitably emergencies; but do not cry wolf (again, little things can be important, if your every email carries a priority symbol it may quickly annoy and will certainly become ineffective)

A common forum for discussions with your boss is the ubiquitous meeting. Making meetings work is a skill that will assist you in many ways; some of the methods of doing so are considered in the next section.

Getting The Most From Meetings

Meetings are much maligned (*Meetings are indispensable when you don't want to do anything*: J. K. Galbraith), but many are necessary, and many may involve you interacting with senior people. If you "work" them well they can play a prime part in allowing you to influence things. This is an area of expertise, amongst others such as presentation, business writing, time management, and more, that is well described, in a phrase used earlier, as a *career skill*. By that I mean a skill that not only allows better performance in a particular job, but which also puts you in a better position in terms of successful career development. [This is a concept that is explored in detail in another book: *Detox your Career*.] To make meetings go well, certain things are important:

- **Always prepare:** read papers circulated in advance,

note the agenda, think about what you want to say, make notes, assemble relevant materials

- **Look the part:** especially in terms of being, and appearing, well organized
- **Clarify:** never participate in discussions if you are not clear about the objectives – ask for clarification (there is no harm in being seen to have things straight before making comments)
- **Handle the discussion:** for example, judge well when to speak and when not
- **Communicate effectively:** preparation helps, but in a meeting, with time pressing, it is important to be "precise and concise" and, above all, always to be clear (your credibility is hardly helped if people are constantly having to clarify what you mean)
- **Obey the rules:** be on time, respect the Chair, observe any necessary formalities, and conduct yourself reasonably and courteously
- **Read between the lines:** people's motivations may be disguised (or their intentions negative or destructive) – watch out too for any politics
- **Display some clout:** be prepared, and ready, to fight your corner, to dig your heels in, or challenge others, and when you do so, have a well-argued and well-supported case – in a way that displays confidence and maintains some courtesy
- **Maintain flexibility:** be prepared, but not locked into a position – meetings are a forum in which you must be quick on your feet

- **Agendas:** if you originate the agenda, make sure
  it relates to the time available. If you find the time
  available has shrunk, you should debate and agree with
  your boss which items will be dealt with and which
  held over until another time
- **Make clear notes:** always be sure you know what has
  been said, what has been decided – and what action
  is required of you (this applies during a meeting and
  from one meeting to the next)
- **Follow up:** action matters agreed, as decided (you do
  not want to be the one shown up at the next meeting
  as having failed to implement action points)

There are skills to develop here, and meetings can be a
stage on which many of your interactions with your boss and
other senior people can be played out successfully – using
meetings wisely and carefully can make a real difference to
your profile and what you can achieve.

LISTENING

Senior people do not want misunderstandings. They do not
want to hear you say, *I'm not quite sure what you meant*
… and they certainly do not want any confusion resulting
from their contact with you to waste any of their time
endlessly repeating things.

As a result, it is important to listen, and to recognize
that this is not quite as simple as it seems. So, be sure to:

- **Listen:** really listen (see the checklist that follows)
- **Ask if in doubt:** and do so immediately (at the end

of a meeting going back and querying something casts doubt on your total understanding)

- **Recap if necessary:** a quick statement – *so this means that ...* – can clarify rapidly and is noticed as nothing other than your being precise and concerned for detail
- **Make notes:** get into the habit of doing so quickly and accurately (and maybe checking them *immediately* after a discussion, filling them out somewhat if necessary, while things are fresh in your mind. After a meeting, when everything has been noted as the meeting progressed, it may be useful to highlight key aspects of what was said; this is simply done using a second color on your notes)

! ● Few skills are so appreciated by senior people as listening. If you listen well, get things right and get them right first time, then your ability to influence is automatically enhanced.

More details designed to hone your listening skills are set out in the checklist below.

Listening Checklist

Make listening an *active* process. The checklist recaps and adds further points, highlighting comprehensively ways to enhance your listening skills. You should:

- **Want to listen:** this is easy once you realize how useful it is to the communication process
- **Look like a good listener:** people always appreciate it if they see they have your attention, and feedback will be more forthcoming as a result
- **Understand:** it is not just the words, but the meaning that lies behind them that you must note
- **React:** let people see that you have heard, understood, and are interested. Nods, small gestures and signs, and comments will encourage the other person's confidence and participation – right?
- **Stop talking:** other than small acknowledgments, you cannot talk and listen at the same time. Do not interrupt (or as an old boss of mine used to put it: *Don't talk while I'm interrupting!*)
- **Empathize:** put yourself in the other person's shoes and make sure you really appreciate their point of view
- **Check:** if necessary, ask questions promptly to clarify matters as the conversation proceeds. An understanding based even partly on guesses or assumptions is dangerous. But ask questions diplomatically; do not say things like *You didn't explain that properly*
- **Remain unemotional:** too much thinking ahead, particularly when you seek to rebut something – *however can I overcome that point?* – can distract you
- **Concentrate:** allow nothing to distract you
- **Look at the other person:** nothing is read more rapidly as disinterest, or being discourteous, than an

inadequate focus of attention

- **Identify key points:** edit what you hear so that you can better retain key points
- **Avoid personalities:** do not let your view of the person you are listening to distract you from their message (this applies to any view you may have: don't assume that everything said by people you like is good sense, or vice versa for people you dislike)
- **Not lose yourself in subsequent arguments:** some thinking ahead may be useful; too much and you may suddenly find you have missed something
- **Avoid negatives:** clear signs of disagreement (even a dismissive look) can make the other person clam up and destroy the dialog
- **Make notes:** do not trust your memory, and, if it is polite to do so, ask permission before writing their comments down

Listening successfully is a practical necessity if you are to excel at your own communication with anyone; in working with senior people it is a prerequisite of success. There is good sense in the old saying that people were designed with two ears and one mouth for a good reason.

Now, it is one thing to hear what others are saying, but are they listening to you?

Ensuring That They Listen To You

All the basic rules of good communication apply. No busy boss, or any other senior person, will have the patience to listen to someone who is unclear or who does not have the courage of their convictions. You need to speak confidently (which comes as much as anything from being clear in your mind that you have sound points to make) and clearly. Hesitancy or uncertainty can quickly destroy a good case, which should be made positively. For instance:

- There is no room for too many words such as *perhaps*, *maybe*, or *I think*. Be positive: *This will work – This is the way forward*, and tell people why

- Bland language, devoid of any distinct meaning, is to be avoided. You should never have a *very practical* plan to suggest; you should never say something is *quite good*. If something cannot be described more powerfully than this, why are you suggesting it? If you find yourself tempted to use this sort of language, question yourself to find a better way of putting something: *why is a plan practical? What makes something worthwhile?* The reasons are what you should be spelling out if people are to want to listen

Apart from having something worthwhile and interesting to say, and making sure that you do not distract from it unwittingly (by being obtuse or verbose, for instance), here is a true golden rule: *Never try to compete with an interruption.* You may be in full flight – your pet proposal is going over a storm – but whatever may interrupt, and many meetings, especially less formal ones, are full of interruptions – *always* pause. It may be the telephone, a visitor, or just the tea trolley on its rounds. It may even just be a moment's apparent distraction for no good real or apparent reason. No matter – whatever it is:

- Pause, and do so at once
- Acknowledge what you are doing – *I'll just wait while ...* and do so assumptively as if what you are doing is as much in their best interests as yours (as indeed it is!)
- Reschedule if necessary (for example, if an unscheduled visitor stays on), but suggest a definite time – *Let's meet again at 3 p.m.* – not just later.
- Recap as you restart and be sure that nothing has been missed in any hiatus

The Chronic Non-Listener

Some bosses never seem to listen, concentrate, or take in what you say. First, if this happens to you and not to your colleagues, then consider whether some or all of the fault might be yours. If you fail to get to the point, waffle, or always pick bad moments, and fail to see that, at that time, you are a distraction, then there may be changes you can make to your own practice to increase the chances of getting a fair hearing.

Alternatively, you can try:

- Checking that it is a good, or at least acceptable, moment (and do not continue against insurmountable odds)
- Always asking open questions: those that cannot be answered with a simple *Yes* or *No*. Thus if you have been through something, suspect that little or no

attention was paid to it, and then ask a question, then the fact that it cannot be answered highlights for both of you that some recapping is necessary

- Asking for a recap. Do not say, *I'm sure you didn't hear a word I said*, but ask whether something is clear (such as *So what deadline are we on?*) as a way of judging how much attention has been paid

- Another method: putting it in writing, for instance

Never leave a meeting, or give up on attempts to get agreement, if you feel a significant part of what you have said was not registered.

> **!** Remember, no communication can properly impress if only a part of it is ● actually heard.

Checking – At The Right Time

The following scene is enacted a thousand times a day in offices up and down the country. A manager is hard at work, concentrating on something important, and there is a knock on the door. They pause. Grudgingly. And a member of their team comes in asking – *What should I do about ...?* You may be conscious of doing this yourself.

Often there is an easy answer and, anxious to get back to the task in hand, they quickly tell you and return to their work. No great harm is done, perhaps. Only a minute or two is wasted. They may feel you should have been able to proceed unaided. But a "do this" answer seemed the quickest way of handling it, so they offer an instant solution and minimize the time it takes.

But is this useful?

The truth is that the easy response to such a situation just creates problems. It may minimize the interruption for the manager in the short term, but it guarantees that the questions – and the annoyance that they bring – will continue; asking and prompting this sort of response teaches you nothing. All this inevitably leads to several results, all better avoided:

- Any attempt to maximize the manager's productivity is doomed in the light of regular interruptions (the more people who work for them, the more often it can happen)
- It may seem like a quick fix for you, but you learn little from the process
- When the boss is not there you may be tempted to delay action until you can ask or, at worst, you do the wrong thing

Two things can help address this situation.

The first thing is proper briefing. Yes, it takes time, but you will never be self-sufficient if you simply do not know what to do or how to do it. So ask for – insist on – a briefing if necessary, extend it if it threatens to be too simplistic and appears to be leaving questions hanging, and try to ensure that when you set off on a project you will not have awkward questions that must be answered along the way.

The second, when you are unclear about something, is

to have a think before you go into your boss's office and ask a question. You may be able to come up with the answer, or you may at least be able to pose a possible solution: *I have got to the implementations stage on the X project, and realize that I am not sure who should see the draft plan. I would think all departmental managers should be copied and will do that unless you say otherwise. OK?* Instead of looking as if you had not given any thought to what you should do, they can see the way you are working and may well only have to say, *That's fine.*

Beyond that, try to decide when a real explanation is necessary. This does not mean simply providing the information you need so that you can take immediate action on something, but also so that you know how to handle such things in future. Then deal with it by scheduling time when it will not annoy and interrupt, and when you will get the thorough briefing you need, and time will happily be given to that.

Being Assertive

Alongside persuasion (more of which later), it is often also politic to adopt an assertive approach, while making sure that doing so is seen as acceptable. Be careful not to be too strident (it can give the wrong signals – of desperation, for instance), otherwise in communicating assertively it helps to:

- **Have the courage of your convictions:** only a well-prepared case can be presented this way, and that means one that is positively put and that provides evidence – more than just *I think* or *I say* …

- **Stick to your ground when challenged:** and back up what you say with facts
- **Avoid circumspection:** do not say *perhaps we should* ... when you mean *we should certainly do* ...
- **Use tone and manner to reinforce your intention:** look and sound as if you mean business
- **Recognise a smokescreen** and not be put off with bluster
- **Keep any argument objective and businesslike:** avoid emotional pleas or reactions

A key strategy when adopting an assertive approach is to be prepared to say: No.

Bosses are important. If Heaven and Earth need moving to keep them happy, then we move them; usually without argument. But is this always right?

Consider the downsides: first, in the heartland of your work area. Say you are recommending that a project be conducted in a particular way. Your boss bemoans the cost of your recommendation. They ask for, perhaps demand, a cheaper option. Under pressure you give in; you recommend – albeit grudgingly – something cheaper, albeit pointing out its shortcomings. If they take the second option and then – surprise, surprise – find it does not do the job properly, then whom do they blame? No surprise here; it is you. And it is completely useless reminding them of your earlier reservations. They will respond by saying something like: *Well, if that was really your view you should have insisted.* And they have a point. If you are to offer your opinion or advice, then doing so necessitates having the courage of your convictions. At worst, not standing up to your boss in this way means their perception of you changes, and next time they may well involve someone else in a project that you see as yours.

An example can illustrate this. In a company I know I saw a boss causing a member of their staff considerable problems. The boss's disorganization was at the root of the problem. They were forever canceling or changing meetings and demanding attendance at others at short notice. They commonly telephoned to demand that the person rush to one of their many regional offices at a moment's notice. This sort of situation cost time and money and ultimately threatened the viability of a carefully costed project. The instinct was to respond helpfully, to manage somehow to accommodate them (after all, it *was* the boss asking). In this case being helpful just compounded the problem.

This boss was of the "give us an inch and we will take a mile and a half" school (*aren't they all?*, you may say). Every helpful act simply made them feel that *anything* demanded would be responded to positively. Ultimately, if demands go up and up, something must be done. But it is a question of degree. Where do you draw the line? Perhaps the best answer is sooner rather than later, despite the instinct to help on each individual occasion; and the real fear that saying no jeopardizes the working relationship.

You have to make saying *No* sound reasonable. Most people are reasonable, even if they act unreasonably. Prompted to think, they do, in fact, realize that their needs are not your only concern, that you have other responsibilities, indeed other commitments. Perhaps they would rate you less highly if you had nothing to do but run after them. If they value your expertise they will know you have other priorities. So if you say *No* and effectively point this out to them, they will not immediately believe this is unreasonable. Thus there is a good deal of difference between just saying you cannot meet at a particular time, and saying that you have a prior commitment, perhaps one involving another project you are handling for them. They would doubtless not want you canceling *their* meetings at short notice, so why should they expect you to do just that to someone else?

Couple this approach with offering an alternative and it becomes even more acceptable: *I cannot ... but I can arrange for one of my colleagues/ I could make the following day.* Your manner here can shape opinion and image; the job is to make them see a reasonable alternative, not to tell them that they are unreasonable (though this may sometimes be a final option).

To return to the earlier example, once the boss there was stood up to, the result was not an explosion. They were nonplussed for a moment, but accepted an alternative and later, having been met with such a response on a number of occasions, gradually became less unreasonable.

Image is both fragile and volatile. Of course, your work and expertise create much of it. And it can be enhanced in particular ways, for example by your ability to make a cracking presentation. But the general day-today communication between you and your seniors also contributes significantly. They surely do not want to deal with a mouse. They expect expertise to be coupled with confidence – in a word "clout." Saying *No* somewhat more often might save you some inconvenience. More importantly, standing up to people when appropriate might well actually improve your standing with them rather than, as you might fear, the reverse.

> **Being assertive only means adopting a planned, positive way of putting over a strong case. Senior people will expect it and respect it.**

Dealing With Emotions
Good grief. How dare you. I've never been spoken to like that in my life. Why you ...

What comes next, whoever may be speaking, could now take the conversation into unwelcome territory. There may be plenty of things in the work environment that make people upset, angry, or worse, but responding in kind will almost always make things more difficult.

The rule is clear: *you must control your emotions.*

To continue while you are incoherent with rage (or in the grips of any other emotion, for that matter) is folly. You will not be thinking logically and the chances of you making a clear point are vanishingly low. Making things worse is much more likely.

Count to ten. Calm down. Focus on the facts, and you

may get somewhere. But you will only do so if you can calm the other person down too. The only alternative is to walk away. If it is you who is upset – and it is apparent – acknowledge the fact and put the conversation on hold: *I'm sorry, but I'm too upset to continue this – Let's talk about it later.*

But what about when it is your boss who is emotional?

The Emotional Boss
The first situation to consider is when your boss shouts at you angrily and you deserve it. There may be better ways for them to do it, but then it may be best to:

- Admit the fault
- Apologize
- Offer any suitable compensatory action (staying on late to do something again, perhaps)

This may well nip the situation in the bud. The point is made, the response is suitable, and the heat evaporates as quickly as it appeared.

Alternatively, the boss may be angry only because they have misunderstood something and you are not in fact at fault. What then?

- Listen and find out what is causing the anger (after all, people get angry because they think it is the only way of making a point. It is not, of course, but not listening is a sure way to heighten their anger)
- Respond positively: that is, accept that what they are saying is something to regret and be angry about

- Then, and only then, point out the misunderstanding and do so in a way that describes factual differences between what they are angry about and what actually happened, rather than just saying: *It's not my fault*
- Action may still be necessary, but now you ought to be able to discuss it rationally

As it becomes clear that the line they took was over the top, they will hopefully feel the need to apologize first, and you may feel that accepting gracefully is the best way to put it all behind you.

Sometimes it proves that the anger is being used tactically to put you under pressure; to get you to agree to something you do not really want, for instance. In this case you must address the tactic promptly and make it clear that it will not work.

- You can say you are not prepared to deal with the matter unless it can be discussed rationally
- If this does not change the approach, threaten to leave: *Let's deal with this later when you have calmed down*
- Do not give time or repeat the threat: leave. You can say *I've made my position clear, I'm leaving*

If the situation continues when you meet later – repeat the formula. No other action will help – you have to repeat as necessary until the situation calms. In the end this action will build a better relationship than rolling over or bursting into tears.

For both parties the only way forward is to head firmly for calm, rational conversation.

Another sort of problem can occur if your boss is emotional, and perhaps with good reason (they are grieving, say, though the cause may be internal or external), and they bend your ear about it. Then:

- Check they really want to talk about it: *It's really none of my business; are you sure you want to tell me?*
- If they insist, then listen (but offer sympathy rather than any advice; even if advice is asked for, it may be better to decline)
- Do not refer to the matter again beyond a bland *How are you?*
- Do not raise the matter again and do not tell others (the last thing you want is it replayed on the grapevine and for it to be clear that you are the only possible source)

! Always aim to deal with business matters in a businesslike and unemotional way, unless, of course, you project positive emotions – there are certainly business matters to be excited or enthusiastic about.

Absence Makes ...

You may work for a boss who is out of the office for much of the time. This reminds me of the story of someone arriving unannounced to see a senior and much traveling manager.

His secretary explained that he was in Hong Kong. The visitor was somewhat exasperated, and commented on the fact that he was out more than he was in, asking: *Who does his work when he is away from the office?* She fixed him with a steely look and replied, *The same person who does it when he's here!* It makes a nice comment on both senior management and secretaries. But I digress.

If you work for someone like this, or indeed are out of the office a good deal yourself, then you need to recognize the fact and organize accordingly. For instance:

- Regular meetings need to be set up around the absences. Time management in the office matters that much more when you effectively only have a part of the full working time in which to arrange things
- Diaries need to be accurate and clear. I once had to contact a fellow consultant because his family was involved in a car accident. I knew he was out for a couple of days conducting a training course. But his diary said only "Oxford" and it took 24 hours to discover exactly where he was and make contact. It gave the whole group an unpleasant lesson to
- Clear guidelines need to be established regarding what necessitates contact being made and what does not. This may involve routine updates about some current project, and it should also usefully define "emergency" so that people know when others need informing about something – in either direction

- Beware particularly of wasting time making or receiving telephone calls just to *see if everything is OK*. The waste here can be enormous, especially now we all have cellphones. Again, the nature of what can or cannot wait must be defined. Just because something is dramatic does not mean that it demands attention. I remember conducting a course for a group of hotel managers. One of them rushed away to take a phone call at lunchtime, returned, and was asked by a colleague what it had been about. He explained that someone had committed suicide in the hotel (evidently something that happens with some regularity), and was asked why he had been called. *There's nothing I can do from here,* he said; *all the procedures have been followed – I suppose they just thought I would like to know.* As for me, I think I would have preferred to know later, especially as I was several hundred miles away – the possibilities of getting involved were nil. Exceptional, perhaps, but it makes a point – what do you need to know and what do you need to tell your boss? Ensure that there is a clear policy

- Once the traveler has returned, schedule a prompt catch-up meeting so that common knowledge and understanding are achieved quickly, and that time is not wasted trying to catch up in an ad hoc fashion from a dozen different sources

This is the kind of area where efficiencies impress the boss, precisely because they address practical problems and make things work. The ubiquitous email is a particularly useful tool in this context.

Overall, communication is key to good relationships with senior people, and some aspects of this need more detailed consideration. Sometimes you are not just telling the boss something, you want their agreement. It is to this that we turn in the next chapter.

06

Getting Agreement from Your Boss

> 66 When I am getting ready to reason with a man, I spend one-third of my time thinking about myself and what I am going to say: and twothirds thinking about him and what he is going to say. 99
>
> *Abraham Lincoln*

The way to get what you want from your boss may be just to ask. If all that is necessary is to ask *Can I do this?* and the answer is *Yes*, then there is no great problem. But what you ask for may well have implications, not least for the boss who agrees it. Ask for additional resources and it will doubtless cost money. Ask for more time and the delay may affect many other things. Ask to change a system or procedure and it may appear to complicate things in another area. Ask for a salary increase and again the implications are perhaps wider than you might think at first sight. If your request is sensible, the result likely useful, and the relationship with your manager good, then asking may be sufficient. But remember that there is a competitive element in play here. Ask for more resources and probably others are doing the same. For the boss it is not just a question of assessing whether your idea is individually worthwhile. It may well be so, but so perhaps are a lot of ideas from others all competing for the same budget. In these circumstances asking may be insufficient. Indeed, a number of factors are involved here, and sometimes something that seems utterly straightforward can cause problems.

Case Study

Consider an example: George runs the sales office for a mediumsized company. His team takes customer enquiries, offers technical advice, handles queries of all kinds, and takes orders. Recent reorganization has resulted in the merging of two separate departments. His people now occupy one large office together with the order processing staff and those who see to the invoicing and documentation. For the most part, all is going smoothly. However, the routing of telephone calls has become chaotic. The switchboard, despite having a note explaining who handles customers in each area of the country, is putting two out of three calls through to the wrong person, and the resulting confusion is upsetting staff and customers alike as calls have to be transferred.

George cannot deal with this himself. Personnel control the switchboard operation. So he carefully drafts and sends an email to the Personnel Director, someone who is at a senior level compared with George. His note complains that the inefficiency of the switchboard service is upsetting customers and putting the company at risk of losing orders. George sees no problem with this; indeed, he assumes a senior person will see the problem and want to sort it out promptly, so he is surprised to find that, far from the situation improving, all he gets is a defensive reply listing the total volume of calls with which the hard-pressed switchboard has to cope, quoting other issues of far more importance at present to the Personnel department, and suggesting he takes steps to get customers to ask for the right person.

George intended to take prompt action that would improve customer service. He felt he had stated his case clearly and logically (and politely), yet all he succeeded in doing was rubbing a senior manager up the wrong way. The problem remained.

Think, for a moment, about how else this might have been handled before reading on. Any ideas?

Here the core of the communication is in writing. The memo George emailed, though well intentioned, had the wrong effect, and would also have made any follow-up conversation (necessary because the problem had still to be resolved) more difficult.

From the way the example is first stated, we can imagine the sort of memo that was sent, probably something along the following lines:

Memorandum
To: Ms X, Personnel Director
From: Mr B, Sales Office Manager

Subject: Customer Service

A recent analysis shows that, since the merging of the sales office and order processing departments, two out of three incoming calls are misrouted by the switchboard and then have to be transferred.

This wastes time and, more important, is seen by

> customers as inefficient. As the whole intention of this department is to ensure prompt, efficient service to our customers, this is not only a frustration internally, it risks reducing customers' image of the organization and, at worst, losing orders.
>
> I would be grateful if you could have a word with the supervisor and operators on the switchboard to ensure that the situation is rectified before serious damage results.

The problem is certainly identified, its implications spelled out, and a solution – briefing of the relevant staff by the Personnel Director – is suggested. The intention, as has been said, is good. However, despite a degree of politeness – I would be grateful ... the overall tone of the message is easy to read as a criticism. Furthermore, the solution is vague: tell the operators what exactly? It seems to be leaving a great deal to Personnel. Maybe George felt "it is not my fault, they should sort it out." To an extent this may be true, but you may find you often have to choose between drawing attention to such a fact or setting out something designed to get something done. They are often two different things.

In this case the key objective is to change the action, and to do so quickly before customer relations are damaged. This is more important than having a dig at Personnel, and worth taking a moment over. While it is a matter of overall company concern, it is of more immediate concern to the sales office.

So what should George have done? To ensure attention, collaboration, and action, his memo needed to:

- Make the problem clear
- Avoid undue criticism, or turning the matter into an emotive issue
- Spell out a solution
- Make that solution easy and acceptable to those in Personnel (including the switchboard operators themselves)
- Perhaps with that in mind, his memo should have been more like the following:

Memorandum
To: Ms X, Personnel Director
From: Mr B, Sales Office Manager

Subject: Customer Service

The recent merger of the sales office and order processing departments seems to have made some problems for the switchboard.

You will find that I have set out in this note something about what is happening and why, and am making specific suggestions to put it right. You will see that most of the suggested action points are for me, but I would like to be sure that you approve before proceeding.

THE PROBLEM
Two out of every three calls from customers coming

into the company are misrouted and have to be transferred. This wastes time both in my department and on the switchboard and is likely to be seen as inefficient by customers. To preserve customer relations, and perhaps ultimately orders, it needs to be sorted out promptly.

THE REASON

Apart from the sheer volume of calls, always a problem at this time of the year, the problem is one of information. The switchboard operators have insufficient information to help guide them, and the departmental merger has outdated what they do have. Given clear guidance neither they, nor customers, will have any problems.

ACTION

What I would suggest, therefore, are the following actions:

1   I have prepared a note (and map) showing which member of staff deals with customers from which geographic area, and would like to make this available for reference on the switchboard.

2   This might be best introduced at a short briefing, and if we could assemble the operators for ten minutes before the switchboard opens one morning, I could do that with them and answer any questions.

> 3   Longer term, it would be useful if the operators visited our department and saw something of what goes on; we could arrange a rota and do this over a few lunch hours so that it can be fitted in conveniently.
>
> If this seems a practical approach, do let me know and I will put matters in hand.

This second memo is not set out as the only "right" or guaranteed approach (much less the exact wording), but it is certainly better. And it is more likely to work because it follows the rules (linking to the various steps set out later in this chapter), namely it:

- Lays no blame
- Recognizes that Personnel, and the switchboard, are important
- Considers their needs – for clear guidance, being able to handle the volume more easily, someone else taking the action
- Anticipates objections: who will do all this, for instance
- Is specific in terms of action, who will do what

There seems every chance it will have the desired effect. Many situations exhibit similar characteristics. All it needs is a clear, systematic approach that recognizes the other person's point of view, and sells the desired action.

In short, this is a more persuasive approach. Now, having considered an example in some detail, let us see what communications techniques help with this sort of thing. Before we get to the details of persuasive techniques, let us put it in context. Two things are important as a preliminary to everything else you do:

- Do not just ask, *persuade*
- Do not give up, *persist*

Persuasion requires particular skills and we are all only too aware that we have sometimes deployed them inadequately. As Olin Miller said, When a person says *"I'll think it over and let you know,"* you *know*. Persuasive techniques are investigated over the next few pages, but first consider persistence.

Persistence at least is easy (though do not become a complete bore by deploying too many approaches), and it should never be underrated – as just one more attempt to get agreement may be the successful one. It is an important technique. So, think about being persistent; go on, think about it, I really want you to, go on, do it – read the next section (then I'll stop insisting). Enough!

The Power Of Persistence

The difficulties here are largely psychological. It is difficult when you have been put off several times (*Leave it for the moment – I can't do anything until after the budget period ends – He's in a meeting*) to raise something yet again. You find yourself wondering what on earth you can do next; devoid of a good idea and wanting (if you are honest) to avoid further rejection, it is all too easy to put off further contact until the moment has past and it really is difficult, or even impossible, to do more. It is worth accepting that often the only problem is the hectic nature of someone's schedule – they are not in fact putting you off in any permanent way, they are just putting off dealing with it now in face of other priorities. So, if you have a case to make, always:

- Continue contact until you are firmly told: *No*, and take everything else at face value (so, if you are told – *after the month end* – assume it means just that and plan to raise it again at the right time, better still getting agreement in advance that you will do so)
- Ring the changes on method – send a note or email, then telephone, then raise it at a meeting
- Remember that some methods are better reminders than others (a telephone can be forgotten in a short time and an email can be deleted in a second)
- Find a creative approach if possible, by making what you do unusual, unexpected, and thus more likely to be memorable

Whilst too gimmicky an approach may be rejected, often a creative idea works well. So get into the habit of exploring what you might do. As an example from my own work, consider this incident. After writing a short book for a specialist publisher, I was keen to undertake another topic for them in the same format. I proposed the idea and got a generally good reaction – but no confirmation. I wrote and telephoned a number of times. Nothing. Always I received a delay or a put-off (you may know the feeling!). Finally, when a reminder of the possibility came up yet again from my follow-up system, I felt I had exhausted all the conventional possibilities, so I sat down and wrote the following:

Struggling author, patient, reliable (non-smoker), seeks commission on business topics. Novel formats preferred, but anything considered within reason – ideally 100 or so pages, on a topic like sales excellence sounds good, maybe with some illustrations. Delivery of the right quantity of material – on time – guaranteed. Contact me at the above address/telephone number or meet on neutral ground, carrying a copy of *Publishing News* and wearing a carnation.

I must confess I hesitated over it a little (this was someone I had only met once), but I signed and posted it. Gratifyingly, the confirmation landed on my desk the following day (and you can now read the result – *The Sales Excellence Pocketbook:* Management Pocketbooks).

Sometimes a slightly less conventional approach can work well, even with a boss. You should not reject anything other than the conventional approach; try a little experiment and see what it can do for you.

Take a considered view of time scale too. For example, in my own work a while ago the contact for one client of mine – one for whom I had done a useful amount of work

– left the organization. Naturally I wrote to them in their new organization, but with no effect. Three years later they approached me and I received the greatest amount of work that I have ever booked in one tranche. During that three years I had contacted them seven times, in various ways, and had had one meeting with them – it had begun to seem pointless, especially toward the end, and it would have been very easy to give up, but persistence paid off. There is a useful moral here:

> ❗ Some things need multiple contacts
> over a comparatively short time, while
> ● others need patience and a resolution
> to raise something at the right moment.
> Persistence is a powerful ally.

Persistence alone may not be enough, of course, and some real persuasion may be called for. To deploy this successfully it helps to understand how people make decisions.

Understanding Decision Making

What happens when you ask your manager to agree to something? Assuming they consider it at all, then it helps in deciding how to put the case if you understand something of the way their mind works. The psychology here is well understood, and the following paraphrases approaches originally set out by psychologists in America. When making a decision, people effectively move through several stages of thinking, which broadly run as follows:

- I matter most. Whatever you want me to do, I expect you to worry about how I feel about it, respect me, and consider my needs and how it will affect me
- What are the merits and implications of the case you make? Tell me what you suggest and why it makes sense (the pluses) and whether it has any snags (the minuses) so that I can weigh it up; bearing in mind that few, if any, propositions are perfect and that I have to weigh the merits of competing ideas
- How will it work? Here people additionally want to assess the details not so much about the proposition itself but about other areas associated with it. For example, you might want agreement to take on, or become involved with, a project. The idea of the project might appeal, but say the timing is coincident with something else, then if this is important the clash might appear to be a minus and, if the case is finely balanced, it could be rejected simply because of that
- What do I do? In other words, what action – exactly – is now necessary? This too forms part of the balance. If something seen during a quick flick through this book in a bookstore persuaded you that it might help you, you may have bought it. In doing so you recognized (and accepted) that you would have to read it and that doing so would take a little time. The action – reading – is inherent in the proposition and, if you were not prepared to take it on, this might have changed your decision

It is after this thinking is complete that people will feel they have sufficient evidence on which to make a decision. They have the balance of pluses and minuses in mind, can weigh up the merits of the case, and they can also compare it with that of any other options they are considering. The diagram on page 104 shows graphically how this works and is a useful image to keep in mind. If you imagine two cases being compared in this way, it is perfectly possible that both are good in terms of their pluses and minuses, but that one just beats the other when they are compared with each other. This emphasizes the need to get every detail right and to make sure you do not sell something short; one more, or less, positive detail can sometimes tip the scales one way or the other.

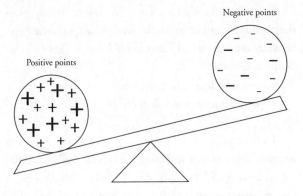

Positive points

Negative points

Remember, your suggestions often relate to other things; if a cost is involved, for instance, on what else might the money be spent? Remember, too, that some choices are close run, with one option only just coming out ahead of others.

> **!** It is this thinking that enables a decision
> ● to be made; and for someone to feel they
> have made a sensible decision, and done
> so on a considered basis.

That said, what can you say about your plan or idea that will make it irresistible? The details matter, but one technique is more useful than any other and is at the heart of the persuasion process.

Persuasion's Magic Formula

People do not agree to ideas or plans in a vacuum or just for the sake of it (and even more rarely just because they like you); they sign up to the *results* of actions or ideas.

The key concept to use here, one taken directly from the world of selling and sales techniques, differentiates between what are called *features* and *benefits*. These we can define as follows:

* Features are the factual elements of something
* Benefits are what it does for, or means to, someone

Thus a crucial factor in achieving agreement is in *talking benefits*. You need to spell out the advantages in specific terms, leading with benefits, describing and stressing those benefits that make the strongest case, and then using features to back up the argument in a way where they demonstrate how it is possible for there to be the stated benefits.

Because this concept is so important, let us examine an example:

Imagine wanting to change a system of some sort (the details of it do not matter). You are sure what you have planned is an improvement. It is less complicated, it can be computerized (rather than being done manually), it is flexible and simple to administer.

As you think it through, ask yourself: *Are these factors features or benefits?*

In this example, things like "able to be computerized" are features; in fact they are all features. What does "being less complicated" mean? (it might mean less thorough). How does running the system on a computer help? What does *flexible* mean, for goodness sake? It is a useful umbrella term, perhaps, but what it implies needs spelling out to give the case weight (it is always dangerous to assume that people will read between the lines and infer exactly the same as you do from a brief description; they are unlikely to do so and the case can be stillborn as a result). Even excellent words like *simple* can fail to do the case justice. If *simple* means that it can be implemented at lower cost by a lower level of staff, saving money and freeing up other people for more important tasks – that needs saying.

In order to ensure that you are focusing on the real benefit when you describe something, always ask yourself what would follow the phrase "which means that ..." Thus if you are just saying something like "simple," adding "which means that" and completing the thought tends to take you to a better, and more persuasive, description.

Using this concept systematically can pay dividends. In fact, what it means is that, rather than simply setting out what you want, which is a one-way process, you are approaching it in a way that is structured to *assist the other person's decision making*. Being persuasive can be defined literally as *Helping someone to make a decision*. Indeed, this is a good way of looking at it. Such an approach is less likely to appear pushy, more likely to be felt to be sensitive to their situation – and thus more likely to get agreement.

> **❗** The rule here should usually be that benefits come first, and that features **●** demonstrate how benefits are made possible.

Benefits come in various forms, so in searching for points to strengthen a case look for benefits:

- **To your manager in their work capacity:** for example, a benefit that means that adopting your idea will improve the productivity of the department
- **To your manager as an individual:** here a benefit might be something that makes life easier, reduces worry, or gives them more time personally
- **To other people (with whom your manager is concerned):** this might mean something that affects their own boss or others in the immediate department or around the organization

These are not mutually exclusive. You can look for and use a "package" of benefits from all the above categories to make a case; just as in the analogy of the balance (see page 99). Every case you make needs to be:

- Sufficiently comprehensively described to have weight and credibility; so the detail is important (especially, as has been said, if you are putting something up in an essentially competitive arena)
- Manageable in the sense that it can be presented succinctly in a reasonable amount of time, and so that making a decision does not become overcomplicated (and likely to be put off) because of the sheer amount of facts to be considered. As a rule of thumb, this implies making five or six main points about something. Each may have an amount to be said about it, but the overall number seems manageable; too few will seem to make the case lack substance, too many can overpower and confuse

Senior people expect no less if they are to judge something presented to them.

> **!** **●** Select the right benefits, describe them clearly, and you have the basis of a strong case and can make agreement more likely.

Even the right, well-described benefits may not do the job; another element is also important.

Adding Weight To A Case

Two further factors can be used to add weight to your argument:

1. **Proof:** that is, any evidence *other than or as well as what you say* (after all, your view might just prompt the feeling that, being in favor of something, you are bound to push it). Thus proof might be someone else's opinion, the results of a test or trial, facts and figures where appropriate – all add weight to the argument from a different perspective and make the time and effort of assembling the evidence worthwhile. Think of the difference if a secondhand car salesman says, *This model will do 40 miles per gallon*, rather than *The test conducted by "What Car" magazine showed that this model will do 40 miles per gallon*. The latter is always going to be more credible. Adding proof boosts the credibility of a case, and also shows that you have taken trouble to assemble the case.

2. **Thoroughness:** and this is meant in the broadest sense. An argument carries more weight when your manner is appropriate. When you have clearly done your homework, when accompanying facts and figures are well explained and well documented, and when the way you put over your case clearly involves good preparation and presentation – all this helps. For example, the poor quality of a presentation or report may condition the response. A reaction may begin and end as *What a rotten presentation, I bet it was a stupid idea anyway*. It is unpleasant to be left in a position

where a negative response has been prompted because you failed to present your ideas properly.

! Always do justice to your requests, and give all your arguments suitable weight.

You can apply these principles to any situation. To illustrate this, let us consider three specific examples and highlight the key factors involved.

1. Asking For A Pay Increase

This is a matter of persuasion if anything is. It is also one where it is very easy to let your personal feelings swamp any attempt to put forward an objective argument.

So first, some dos and don'ts:

Do not say: *I've been working very hard, I have been here a long time, X got more money so I should too*, do not quote a friend in another organization, and never plead poverty due to personal circumstances that have nothing to do with work (*I'm moving house, having a baby, planning a special holiday*). Also do not threaten, demand, or become emotional.

Over and above maintaining an ongoing payment level (due to inflation), there may be good reasons for a rise, so do say if you have:

- Increased your responsibilities or the breadth of your operational area in same way
- Saved the organization money

- Worked longer or more unsociable hours
- Traveled or stayed away more frequently
- Achieved new qualifications or skills
- Become more self-sufficient
- Increased your contribution (with ideas, for instance)
- Exceeded expectations or targets in terms of tangible results

Fit your request with any prescribed review processes where possible, but then – or whenever you need to push – do so confidently and assertively (the worst answer is perhaps No, in which case plan – agree? – when you can best ask again). Additionally, you probably need to be prepared to respond to something that appears to be other than the final offer or response – negotiation may be another technique you need to deploy here (and is another useful career skill, one we touch on at the end of this chapter).

 Be objective, be factual – and stay calm.

As a final thought, a creative approach might work. In an idle moment a boss of mine once told me he had himself obtained a pay rise by saying he would have to work harder that year as it was a leap year. I waited more than two years until the next one to remind him – and delivered a moment of amusement and got a small extra increase as a result!

2. Asking For More Responsibility Or Promotion

Everyone wants their job to allow them to make progress; indeed, the concept of the need for active career management is widely accepted (and explored in *Detox your career*, which is another book I have written). There are two possible routes here. Firstly, responsibility can be added piece by piece until the whole job has become rather different. At that point the cumulative body of changes may need formalizing.

Secondly, one can move straight to a significant change – a promotional step up.

Both are integral parts of active career management. The piece-bypiece route is helped by such interim approaches as encouraging delegation and taking initiatives.

To get things formalized, the best approach is similar to asking for an increase in your remuneration: it should be objectively and factually based – not an emotional plea – *but I've been here three years!* What you are trying to do is show how the organization, and maybe your boss in a personal sense too, would benefit if what you do is reconfigured. The decision-making process is as much in evidence here as with anything else. You need to lay out and stress the benefits of what you suggest. You also need to recognize that there may be downsides: who will take on tasks you are suggesting you move away from, for instance? Bringing solutions to such snags to the table is part of presenting a powerful case. This applies as much if you are going for a shift in your present job as it does if you are looking for an actual promotion into a new job.

One possible danger here is the tendency of people to underrate their own competence. I can think of one person who just six months into a job found their boss taking early retirement on health grounds. The position was two grades up, and this, plus their limited time in their existing job, seemed to militate against their applying. But, when with some encouragement they did, they found that their total experience, together with the impression they had made even in only six months, got them the job. There seems to be a clear moral here: aim high (and keep your C.V., and all that you need to back up this kind of application, up to date).

Just one other thing to keep in mind. Most organizations are concerned about fairness (because it's, well, fair – and unfairness on staff matters can all too easily overlap into employment legislation and cause major, time-consuming, and costly problems). So, while you should probably not make demands solely because of this, a need to be fair may sometimes appropriately be a logical part of a reasoned argument.

Incidentally, the prevailing view of what constitutes fairness in some areas changes in line with other circumstances and legislation. For example, sustained pressure for fair treatment of women during pregnancy and after birth has resulted in statutory maternity leave, something that is costly to employers and yet is regarded as a better arrangement by many people. At the same time, other people – single, childless, or with grown-up children – complain that the fact that someone is off for months looking after a new baby while they cover for them is unfair, especially if they cannot get even one day off for something else, like visiting a sick relative. Perhaps it is too much to hope that there will ever be a complete consensus about such things. Even so, when you act on the basis that something is "not fair," do make sure you see the broad picture and are not just saying, I don't like it.

3. Training And Development

Training is generally seen as a good thing. Certainly in today's dynamic workplace you will want to take advantage of any development activity that you can. However, restraints on time and money may interfere and mean you get less sanctioned than you believe would be useful to you (and to your organization, of course). An old maxim quotes a manager saying: *What if I invest time and money training my people, and then they leave?* The answer is another question: *What happens if you don't train them – and they stay?* If your boss has any sense, they will want everyone working for them to be effective, recognie that they must have the right skills, and ensure that those skills are kept up to date.

Even so, it is perfectly valid for you to take some initiatives in this area, but here again a good case needs to be made – you are asking your boss to see money being spent and, if you are to attend a course, for you to be absent from your post, with all the inconvenience that may cause them, and others. They need persuading.

So, key ways to make your training suggestions acceptable include:

- **Stressing the benefits:** primarily this will involve

the way you will be able to perform your job after training (be as specific as possible and remember that immediate benefit tends to make a more powerful argument than longer-term ones)

- **Focusing on results:** not just *I will be able to write better reports*, but *My reports will do a better job for the department*, and then spelling out how

- **Being practical:** it is inherently more difficult to organize a month out of the office than a couple of days at a seminar (for instance, an idea such as finding a like-minded group and suggesting an in-company program, which might be cost effective compared with lots of people attending different external programs, might find merit – so take the broad view)

- **Offering proof:** (such as benefits experienced by others) and utilize the support of others where appropriate (the training manager, perhaps)

- **Mixing the topics of training:** some specific and task based, others perhaps more career focused. This may be a way of including topics that might be difficult to get agreement on in isolation

Two different categories of training may be relevant here. Firstly, there are those skills that your boss knows you could improve. For instance, if every time anything you write drops on their desk they make a point of mentioning its lack of clarity, structure, and the minuscule amount of punctuation it contains, then suggesting that you book in for a course on business or report writing may immediately seem logical (though it still has to be fitted in and paid for).

Secondly, if you are asking for something less obviously beneficial – maybe you want to get training in presentational skills, not because making presentations is something you currently do, but because you hope that your job will develop in a way that will make this a useful skill in the future – then the task of persuading your boss is likely to be more difficult.

All such examples make the same point: the instinctive I want kind of approach is not automatically likely to succeed. To put over a convincing case needs care and consideration – and it needs doing in a way that matches well with the person making the decision. You are not telling them what to do; you are helping them make the right decision. Thought of and approached in that way, your case is more likely to be agreed. It helps too if you are known to undertake some self-development: reading some business books, utilizing a corporate resource centre, logging on to internet training, and more. You are seen to be doing what you can, and the organization may see you as worth spending more on. If, during your self-development activity, you cross paths with a training manager, and can perhaps quote their view as evidence, that may help too.

Another thing that may help extend training opportunities, especially when your boss sees them as time consuming, is to find ways to fit them in with normal day-to-day work. On one occasion I saw a dramatic improvement in presentations skills where a group of people suggested to their boss that in certain meetings their contributions were made more formal. For a period it was agreed that they would stand up and address the meeting in a presentational style, and this was coupled with some critique afterward. The boss was thus able to assist development on this topic in a way that cost no money and needed very little extra time. As a side effect of such ideas, seeing something work may help produce permanent change; the boss sees that skills can be improved without too much hassle, and if the improvement is useful then they consider the next idea more favorably.

A final point on this topic: always provide feedback. For instance, many organizations have a mandatory feedback form, which must be completed after a course is attended. Always complete it and copy it to your boss whether or not they have asked you to do this. If there is no form, write a note: tell them about the course, say how it was useful, and, above all, say how you think it will affect what you can do in the future. It is always nice, too, to end it with a *Thank you*.

Beyond Persuasion – Negotiating With The Boss

Sometimes being persuasive is not enough. Let us be clear. Negotiation and persuasion are different things. They are certainly interrelated: successful persuasion gains agreement to action, negotiation is concerned with identifying, arranging, and agreeing the terms and conditions that accompany agreement. Thus, in the training example above, you might persuade your boss that you need training in a particular skill, but then negotiate about how this is dealt with, when, and at what cost. Agreement must logically come first. People do not waste time negotiating something in which they have no interest.

Consider three factors about negotiation:

1. **Negotiation is a complex process.** The complexity comes from the need to orchestrate a multi-faceted process rather than because of anything individually intellectually taxing. But you need to be quick on your feet to keep all the necessary balls in the air, and always see the broad picture while concentrating on individual details.

2. **Negotiation must not become an argument (otherwise an impasse usually results).** But it *can be* adversarial. Both parties want the best deal possible. Yet compromise is essential: stick out for the perfect deal and the other party may walk away. Give way too easily and you will regret what is then agreed. What is sought is the so called *win-win* outcome, where both parties are satisfied, and, while neither may have their ideal "best deal," they each have an agreement about which they feel comfortable.

3. **Negotiation has a ritual aspect.** A process needs to be gone through. It takes time. There is to and fro debate, and it must be seen that a mutually agreeable solution is being sought. Too much haste, a rush for agreement, or a take it or leave it approach can fail simply because the other party does not feel that the process is being taken sufficiently seriously. They look for hidden

meaning, believe that something better must be possible, and again the outcome can be stalemate.

Because of these factors the best negotiators are careful to take the broad view, to understand the other person's viewpoint, what they are trying to achieve, and why. Because the issues and motivations of negotiation are complex, the way it is handled is important. In addition, the negotiator who seems confident, dealing with all the issues logically, and managing the overall process as well as picking up the detail, commands respect. How do you get on top of it all to this extent? Well, beyond having a clear understanding of the process, the key is preparation. You cannot just wing it.

The rule about preparation is simple. Do it. Preparation may only be a grand term for the age-old advice that it is best to engage the brain before the mouth, and it may take only a few moments; but it could take longer – it is always worthwhile.

Clear objectives are vital. Simply saying, *I want the best deal* possible provides nothing tangible with which to work. There is all the difference in the world between my saying, *Let's see if I can get the boss to give me more responsibility* and aiming *to be allowed to write the X report myself.* Planning should be designed to produce the equivalent of a route map, something that helps shape the meeting. With people it is just not possible to predict everything exactly as it will happen. However, your plan should provide both an ideal route forward *and* a basis to help if things do not go exactly to plan.

A final point may also encourage you to spend time

preparing. You must *appear* well prepared. If it seems obvious you are unfamiliar with the issues – more so if this is actually so – then it is more likely someone will run rings around you. Preparation is the foundation to success and insurance against being outclassed.

The core of the negotiation process revolves around what are called variables: factors that can be dealt with in different ways to create various deals. Thus in negotiating salary, say, you may need to involve other things: pension and bonus payments, expenses, holiday entitlement, company car, and more, plus factors such as timing.

The overall rules here include:

- Aiming high, going for the best deal possible
- Discovering the full list of variables the other person has in mind
- Treating *everything* as a potential variable
- Dealing with detail within the total picture (rather than one point at a time without reference to others)

Various ways of using variables can increase the power from which you deal. For instance, you can prompt attention by offering *reward*: something you are prepared to give. Conversely, you can offer *punishment*: by flagging your intention to withhold something. Your case is strengthened, given *legitimacy* in the jargon, by being supported by factual evidence, or by the use of *bogeys*, peripheral factors included only to distract or seek sympathy.

You have to rank the variables, in preparation and in fine-tuning, as you go, identifying things that are:

- Essential: you cannot agree any deal without these points being part of it
- Ideal: what you intend to achieve (and the priorities, because there may be more of these than it is realistic to achieve)
- Tradable: in other words, those things that you are prepared to give away to help create a workable deal

The concept of *trading variables* is key to negotiation. Aim never to *give anything away*. Concessions (variables given away) must be traded – *I can certainly get that done by the end of the week, but it will mean delaying that other job*. In trading, the value of every concession must be maximized when you give it – and minimized when you accept it. Thus saying: *I suppose I could do that, though it will make more work, but OK*, makes it seem that what you are agreeing is worth more than perhaps it is. While saying: *I would never normally do this* implies you are making an exception in their favor. And saying: *Well, I suppose if I do that you won't need to ...* exemplifies the effect that the concession has for them. Clearly *how* such things are said, perhaps incorporating some exaggeration, affects their reception.

Similarly in minimizing the other parties' concessions. These can be dismissed – *Fine, now next ...*; belittled – *Well, that's a small point out of the way*; amortized – *I suppose that saves a little each month*; taken for granted – *I would certainly expect that*; or otherwise reduced in power by the way they are accepted and referred to during the discussion.

So, discussion has to be planned, directed, and

controlled. The confidence displayed during it is significant (and links back to preparation). You must be clear about what you want to achieve. If you utilize every possible aspect of the discussion and treat it as a variable, and deploy appropriate techniques to balance the whole picture and arrive at where you want to be (or somewhere close) – then you can achieve a reasonable outcome. Remember the win–win scenario. The job is not to take people – least of all your boss – to the cleaners. If you are only prepared to agree something that is weighted heavily in your favor, negotiation may break down, and no agreement at all may result or your boss will change the game and simply say, *Do this!* Indeed, you must recognize that sometimes walking away, rather than agreeing something you cannot live with, is the right decision.

Do not underestimate the individual techniques that can be deployed. A confident negotiator may use many different ploys to enhance their case. Some are simple, such as the use of silence, which many find embarrassing, to make a point or prompt a response. Too often someone will ask something like *how important is this to you*? They wait a moment and then continue – *well, I'm sure it must be an important factor, now let's* ... This produces no real impact and, more importantly, no information. Wait, wait a long time if necessary (try counting to yourself, a pause that seems long and unsustainable may be only a few seconds). But using – really using – silence is one significant ploy that can help the negotiating process. I bet some readers have bosses who use this technique.

If you negotiate well you can gain considerably; it can affect the package of tasks making up your job, your rewards, and your relationship with your boss. A good negotiator is respected. Negotiating needs care and consideration; it is certainly a career skill and one that can powerfully assist your relationships with senior people.

So much for the principles of communication. Clearly, good communication, and particularly a precise ability to be assertive, to persuade, or to negotiate with your boss, stands you in good stead as you build a relationship, but not everything is straightforward – next we look at some of the difficulties that can arise.

07

Dealing with Difficulties

> 66 There is always an easy solution to every human problem – neat, plausible ... and wrong. 99
>
> *H. L. Mencken*

At this point we address a series of situations and see how some of the many possible difficulties of dealing with an awkward boss can be resolved. These situations are selected both because they are valuable in their own right – they are matters that seem to crop up regularly – and also because they are good examples of the kind of thinking and approach that are required.

The Boss From Hell

Bosses come in every shape, size, and form. Let us hope that yours is not irredeemable, but – like most – they probably have some characteristics that do make for some difficulty, if only on occasion. Firstly consider some general points. Faced with a potential difficulty, always:

- Identify the problem and try to ascertain *why* it is occurring (again, just ask?)
- Be careful not to overreact, especially doing so simply with immediate, visible irritation
- Approach any problem sensitively and use all your

communications skills

- Plan your response, if necessary see changing things as a campaign that may take some time, and do not aim for an "instant fix" (which may not be possible)

The idea of a campaign is worth a further word. At courses I conduct people regularly raise problems. Some are real, others largely imagined, but they need sorting out. Equally regularly, I find that in seeking a solution, only short-term measures have been considered: the issue remains unresolved and is raised with me because no instant answer has been found. The first thing is sometimes to recognize and accept that there is simply no instant fix for everything. In particular, it takes longer to change attitudes than it does simply to pass on and add to the store of information that someone has.

The process of getting a problem accepted as such, getting a solution considered, tried and found to make something work better – and the change to habit, attitude, and perhaps prejudice needed along the way – may well take time. So be it. If that is the nature of the beast, act accordingly. Wishing there was a quicker solution and meantime doing nothing should not be an option.

> **!** Remember, bulls in china shops usually cause more damage than anything else – softly, softly may often be the (only) way.

Do Not Assume Major Problems Where They Do Not Exist

Whatever difficulties you face in dealing with your boss, it is best never to automatically assume things are complicated. Sometimes problems are caused by sheer ignorance. Something is done unthinkingly, or for what seem good (though ultimately inappropriate reasons), and can be corrected very easily.

How? *You just ask.*

Example: Years ago I remember a case of getting regular statistical information. The information was necessary. It allowed me to complete a task I enjoyed. But its format necessitated some sorting out. My boss had never asked how it should best be provided, and it subsequently turned out that he honestly felt the existing format was ideal.

The answer? A simple request – *I wonder if you could* ... backed up with an example of how it could be better arranged, and a brief explanation about how that would save time – eceived instant agreement. A permanent change in practice followed and no additional effort was necessary to produce the information in the revised format.

Sometimes such questions are not asked out of fear. We worry about what a senior person will say: will they bite our head off? Is there a good reason for something that we have not thought of? Think about it, of course, but often, that done, a question causes no problem. As an example, a sales manager was concerned that product information passed to him was unsuitable as a means of briefing his sales team. They needed not just the facts and figures, but also the ability to stress the benefits to potential customers. Reworking the information took time and, as many products and product changes were involved, it took a great deal of time. For a while they put off broaching the subject because the source was very senior. But finally they did, explaining how something differently presented would be much more useful, and why this was so, and providing an example of the different format. I remember this situation primarily because of what I was told happened next. There was no problem and the message came back: *Of course, it can be done like that – why ever didn't you say something earlier?* This sort of thing does not always happen, of course, but often it will do so if you do not rule out the possibility and treat the situation as if it was a major issue.

> **!** ● If it is not a problem, do not treat it like a problem (just make it easy to agree a change).

Now, some specific problems:

The Boss Who Is Secretive

First, you need to accept that there are things that your manager knows that you do not, either because it is inappropriate or not necessary (you could probably spend all day just exchanging details, after all).

But if some sorts of information are withheld then this can make your job more difficult; it may also be a sign that you are being underrated. If there *is* a habit you need to try to change, resist the temptation to gripe or complain vaguely about things in general. Rather, raise it as an issue – one where positive improvement may come from a change – and in doing so:

- **Be specific**: discuss particular things where your lack of knowledge about something has caused problems; and be specific about the problems too – have matters been delayed or costs increased, perhaps as a result of you not being party to something?
- **Gather evidence**: show why it affects you (other than being irritating) and what results from it
- **Emphasize the plus side**: spell out the advantages of more openness, suggesting "improved information flow," rather than "stopping being secretive"
- **Involve others**: because the habit of secrecy may affect other people as well as yourself, get everyone to engage in the same sort of action to rub in the message

Link this to a continuing focus on the problem. Some gentle reminders as other business and communications occur between you should cause no problem if your initial raising of the matter is carefully done and generally well received. You may also get some clarification along the way as to why certain information cannot be disseminated further; if they are good reasons, you may simply have to learn to live with it.

! ● Finally, do not respond in kind and be secretive yourself; your good example may help.

The Boss Who Will Not Delegate

You might think that delegation is a good way for the boss to free up time and involve and develop others. It is. But not undertaking sufficient delegation is a common fault in managers. If this is happening to you, then the first job is to recognize that there are many possible reasons (beyond sheer cussedness!) why a manager may be bad at delegation. If you can then discover what these reasons are, this may prove the first step to changing matters for the better. Major reasons for not delegating include:

- Fear that the process is time consuming (if this is a factor, then using something as an example to demonstrate that you can pick things up and take over fast may help)
- Fear that something will go wrong and they will be blamed (if you can ensure that you do well in what you take over, trust may remove this in time)
- Fear that you will do something *better* than them (well, so you might, but then perhaps you should describe it as being done differently rather than better)
- Hanging on to things which, although appropriate to delegate, they *like* doing (find them something else more important or more satisfying still for them to do)

Any progress here depends on a starting point. If you

can get something delegated and use what happens as an object lesson in the benefits of delegation, then you will begin to change what has perhaps become a habit. A step-by-step approach is often best here, but if this does not work it is a key area, one that may prompt you to examine the long-term benefit of the person as a boss.

> **! ●** Discovering the reason and dealing with it is more likely to change things than just making a general complaint.

The Boss Who Interferes

Whatever you do, you no doubt wish to be left to get on with it. Some things need consultation or support, but constant checking up (or, worse, changing the rules as the game progresses) is a very different matter. This is a sign of the control freak and it usually goes along with an inability to delegate. The only antidote is to ensure that they *build up confidence in you*; show them that all does go well and that this happens reliably even without their monitoring every moment.

Specific action on your part might include:

- Supplying progress reports or arranging discussions ahead of being asked
- Creating regular continuity of contact; gaps will simply encourage unnecessary contacts
- Working to a plan you can describe (this not only shows that all is well, but also indicates that it will continue to be so)

- Sticking to the brief (later you can aim to make changes, but get their confidence built up first)
- Dealing with any checks, even unscheduled ones, objectively and factually and do not let your irritation show
- Making sure that you can *always* quote chapter and verse on what is happening *at any time*

! **Be patient about interference – this needs a campaign to cure it.**

If such checks consistently show that everything is well and you point this out, then gradually confidence will rise and the incidence of unnecessary checks will decline. In addition, you can use diversionary tactics, taking the chance of an unwanted contact to steer the conversation to something more useful; though be careful – if it looks as if you are avoiding a check for the wrong reasons it can make matters worse.

The Boss Who Resists Change

There can often be some ambiguity about change. We all view the concept of change as a good thing in isolation, but can quickly become suspicious if someone comes into our office and says, *There must be some changes here!* Again, it helps if you can work out the reason why this resistance is occurring with your boss. If it is for one major reason you may be able to tackle it. For example, maybe they are frightened of new technology (a problem often made worse by having younger staff who are not). If so, maybe you can offer them help (pick something straightforward you know is a problem and offer some assistance; maybe you can even become seen as a source of regular help). Be sensitive about this approach, however; it must be done tactfully or you can end up making them feel even more inadequate about something.

Many reasons for resisting change are possible; maybe they are just busy, stubborn, or old-fashioned, reacting against anything that upsets their existing ways, in which case you must find ways that fit each case. For example, if they are busy, then you may have to demonstrate that time spent to instigate a change will save more time thereafter; indeed, this is commonly the case. If there is no good reason not to change other than existing habits or prejudices, then you may have to assemble an overpowering case, one which presents so many benefits that it becomes irresistible. Again, a campaign may be necessary to cure this sort of thing.

> **!** **Do not fight people who resist change;**
> **you will add stubbornness to resistance**
> **● – work with them to change their**
> **attitude.**

Three particular tactics may help here:

* *In making suggestions, separate the process of change from the results of making the change.* What is feared or resented is often just the inconvenience of

making the change – sell the results (benefits) and
reactions may be different; minimize the hassle,
which may well be overestimated, and your case is
made stronger still

- *Assist – indeed, enliven – their imagination.*
Describe *how* things will be after a change, and
paint an attractive and truly descriptive picture
- *Do the groundwork.* Make agreeing to the change
consist of saying yes to the results, not yes to a
difficult process of sorting everything out

All three of the above make getting agreement easier.
Afterward (thinking of next time), do not try to take all the
credit – even if it is rightfully yours! If they made a good
decision, it does no harm to say so. You are a team, right?

It may put things in perspective here to realize how
common, and how perennial, this problem is. Almost three
hundred years ago, Samuel Johnson wrote: *Change is not
made without inconvenience, even from worse to better.*

The Boss Who Lays Blame On You

If blame is laid on you unfairly, especially perhaps when it
actually lies with the boss, this is something that you must
tackle; the alternative may be your boss thinking you are a
pushover, and others, more widely, thinking that you are
inefficient.

If this is happening, you may need to:

- Get more instructions in writing, even putting
things in writing yourself – a "this is what I am

doing, is that right" kind of memo; the boss only
has to say *Yes* to this and you have evidence of
what was agreed
- Raise the issue with your boss. Simply redirecting
the blame to them may inflame matters, but do
not accept the blame – it may help to discuss
something less personally: accepting that
something did not go well but referring to both
parties – *We could have done better with this one*
- Avoid switching the blame onto your boss in public;
if they lose face then they may become much more
adamant; other people may not know who to believe
and the whole situation will get messy

This is an unpleasant characteristic and one that should
not be allowed to continue unchecked, but it needs dealing
with carefully.

The Boss Who Is Rude/Abrupt

It is possible that someone's rudeness may be intractable;
if so, you may decide to learn to live with it, and assume
no great harm is intended. Alternatively, its impact may be
either wholly unintentional, or at least something that they
are unaware hurts to the extent it does. If so, then a simple
request may suffice to prompt a change.

If not, then you have to mount a campaign. The kinds
of things that might usefully contribute to this include:
- Setting a good example with your courtesies to
other people (and prompt your boss also where

possible, for example drafting a "thank you" letter
for them to sign)

- Referring to behavior linked to other people – *I
  know John's secretary really hates being called that –
  if you used her proper name, I'm sure we'd get more
  cooperation* – preferably, as shown here, in a way
  that shows some practical advantage to behaving
  differently

- Asking for advice about related matters – *How do
  you think I can approach Mary about that without
  offending her?* Such comments may make a point or
  simply help you detect the reason for behavior you
  find inappropriate

- Ignoring it, then make it clear what you are doing
  – *Sorry, I ignored you: I couldn't believe you were
  talking to me like that*

If you wear them down in this way, they should
eventually take the hint (they may even say *thank you*!). The
worse the outburst the more you should refuse to be drawn
in and play their game. When toddlers have a tantrum there
is no reasoning with them. Ditto bosses – the moment must
be allowed to pass, then communication can be restarted on
a different basis.

If the rudeness humiliates you in public this too is a
serious matter. Do not row with them; that will simply
make matters worse. But do not roll over either; it may
calm the moment but it will not stop them having another
go on another occasion.

So:

- Make sure you do not give them any ammunition. If you have made a monumental blunder, maybe you should expect it to be talked about publicly (though a good boss will rarely do so)
- Be assertive, but be objective and accurate. If the boss says, *Late again for a meeting, I wonder how much time you waste for us all,* they are implying a bad record. If this is simply not true, demand specifics: *I know I was late back from a client meeting last time this committee met, but George is our biggest client – I can't remember being late on any other occasion recently. What occasions do you mean?* If they cannot answer, and if you are right they will not be able to, this will leave them without a leg to stand on and is likely to put them off such tactics

Note: if the upset is *intended*, the same tactics may work. In bad cases you need to check why it is happening. For example, it could be an alternative to meeting some issue head on, or a sign of a deep incompatibility that makes you need to consider your future. In addition, the line between rudeness and actual intimidation or bullying is a fine one; it also takes us into territory where, if the rudeness takes the form of racial, religious, or sexual comments, then these days the law has something to say about it. There will be more said about this later.

The Boss Who Will Not Back You Up

The good boss sees himself or herself as responsible for creating a good team. They need to provide briefing, training, and a plethora of support in all sorts of ways. If they begrudge necessary support, especially something patently obvious to everyone, then you need to raise the issue.

The best way of doing so is to focus on results and on the overall picture; do not say, *I want* ... but rather explain (in writing if the formality will help) why you need something in terms of the results it will bring. For example, you could explain that you will be able to

take on something new or do something faster and more efficiently if you have help, resources, training, or whatever else you need.

Do not be put off by vague promises. Ask for a commitment: what will be done, when will it be done, and how? The case you make here can be positive; *If you do this then ... (something good)*, or negative – fear inducing; *If you don't do this then ... (something bad)*. Either way, you are making it clear that the desired outcome is only possible if the backup is there.

If you win here, remind them later, *All done and that deadline hit. And I'd never have done it without your backing. Many thanks for that.* Do this in a way that helps set things up for the future.

The Boss Who Says "Leave It With Me"

Who has not at some time suffered from this response to a request for action or decision? The tone here may imply that this is a helpful comment – but then you never hear another word. Everyone is allowed to forget something once in a while, but if this is a situation that recurs – and sometimes it is a prime characteristic of a boss – then it certainly demands action. The solution is often straightforward:

- Agree to the comment, but then always ask for (or, better still, suggest), and then agree, a follow-up date so that you can check with them on that date rather than waiting for them to mention it to you again. This should be done whether it is the sort of thing where such a time is a few hours, days, or months ahead

- Make the suggestion of a follow-up date sound convenient to them rather than to you (*to save you time, why not let me ...*)

- Stress the benefits of the matter being dealt with promptly rather than delayed. Do not just go on about *your* situation; describe how this will assist *them*

- Do not let an outstanding matter lie. If no answer is forthcoming on the follow-up date set, then set another (and, if necessary, another!). Be persistent and try to link things to other timing (for example, *let me check with you on the 25th, we should have things sorted out before the end of the month, don't you think?*)

- Offer to get involved in the process of consideration and take on some part of any task involved (for example, *why don't I get the figures out, then all you have to do is ... and by the 25th we should have it all settled)*

- Consider making it public by referring to other people who are/seem aware of the delay (*so, I told John I could start X once I have your decision about Y*)

With the worst examples of this, the key is *persistence*. A dawning realization that you will not forget or give up your reasonable approach should wear them down; your task is to build up good habits. Your persistence is always assisted if they know that it really is something that needs doing and that it should not be put off. The worst case concerns things that are difficult. Very few difficult things are made easier by delay, and yet prevarication is a common fault (you may do it too). We spend time rationalizing that something will come along to change the situation and make it easier, when a moment's real thought shows that this is wishful thinking and action is needed now. You might point this out; but do so tactfully. You might also find that, as the person concerned knows this is so if they think about it, then at the end of the day they actually appreciate your insistence.

The Boss Who Never Consults

Let us be clear what we are talking about here. Various discussions with your boss may be useful: you brief them, they brief you, and so on – but consultation implies something more. By consultation I mean conversations where you work together, where your view is sought, and the discussion combines the expertise of both parties in the hopes of arriving at a thoroughly thought-through view, often one that can best be described as creative. As such this is a vital part of your involvement with a boss, and one that can contribute disproportionately to job satisfaction. If this is something that your boss is currently disinclined to do, it is a prime target for change. The problems causing non-consultation can be similar to non-delegation (fear or lack of time, for instance – dealt with on page 124).

The solution is to demonstrate how useful consultation can be – to them and to the operation (and to you too, of course, though just making things better for you may not be an argument that succeeds on its own). Yet consultation takes some time, and in a busy – pressurized – life this may be seen as a major problem.

The concept that can persuade them is that, by investing time *now*, you can save time later. You can start in small ways. And you can start by taking the initiative rather than just requesting that *they* consult. So:

- Ask – *can we take five minutes on this? I think it would be useful if I understood ...*
- Tell – *one possible problem with this new project is X; I've got a way round that, I think; can we discuss it for a few minutes?* (*there may be other ways in which I could help*)
- Demonstrate – if there are a number of people involved, then reporting on the benefits of *your* consultations with others (down the line, perhaps) may strengthen your case

- Consult with others – *I had a chat with James about X. It was very useful, but you are really the prime mover here, maybe we should ...*
- Use small successes to build the habit. Show how well one thing worked and sell the benefits of "more of the same"

If you are an effective person (would you be reading this if you were not?), then your boss will discover that consultation with you is useful.

> **!●** The trick to organizing adequate consultation is to get the process started, and to demonstrate the benefits so that your boss will want to use it more.

The Boss Who Wants A Cover-Up

A boss/employee relationship is not just a matter of dealing with routine work matters. You can become politically involved in their plans and schemes. This can create a different class of difficulty. For instance, what do you do if your boss asks you to cover up for them? It might be something to do with work or private life (for example, the kind of subterfuge involved in hiding an affair). Leaving the odd white lie aside, for most people *not* being involved in such things is only right. You certainly need to think beyond the immediate implications. Something may not cause problems the first time, but as you become more and more involved there will be more for you to explain if things go wrong. What seemed like loyalty at the beginning provides but a lame excuse later when someone is asking why you kept quiet.

So, bad cases need addressing head-on:

- Raise the issue formally and explain how uncomfortable it makes you feel and what a difficult situation it might create at a later date
- Suggest, if possible, another way (*if they never telephoned the office, I would know nothing about it*)
- Stick to your objective of not being involved, but do not moralize (your intention is to prevent your involvement, not stop whatever it is from happening – though you may want to do that too. If so, that is a separate issue)
- Most people recognize that this sort of thing is wrong, and therefore agreement to avoid it should be attainable. If not, then if the issue is really sensitive you must consider whether in the long term you want to work for such a person

Really serious situations – whistle-blowing incidents perhaps involving money, deception, or more – go beyond the scope of this book. (Suffice to say that you should proceed with caution, take advice from someone who can be objective about the matter, and initially consider acting only in a way that keeps your involvement confidential.)

More often, this is really only a question of both parties knowing, and agreeing to draw an appropriately placed line. Minor incidents should cause no ongoing problem, but if the problem involves major issues or is endemic then it is something about which to think seriously.

This takes us on to matters that are hopefully exceptional but which are also more serious.

Dealing With Serious Problems

There are interpersonal problems that are so grave that they negate the whole boss/subordinate relationship. These include bullying, sexual harassment, and discrimination of any kind (racial, age, gender, religious ...) from your boss or others, and all must be addressed very seriously.

- Firstly, check – and check very carefully – that your worst fears are true and that what is happening cannot be any kind of misunderstanding. Do this objectively; it is very easy to find you are being somewhat paranoid about something about which you are sensitive or about which perhaps you have had, or know of, similar problems in the past. Keep an open mind while you do this thinking and checking and involve your organization's consultation processes as necessary

- Accuracy is paramount, so as soon as you recognize something you wish to contest keep careful records, keep them factual and remember to note times and dates

- Consider carefully what you want to do. There are various options, ranging from organizing for someone else (maybe your boss's boss) to intervene, to taking legal action; or just walking away. You have to balance what could be done with the practicalities of doing it, and include a longer-term career view in your thinking. It is not suggested that you put up with anything of so serious a nature, but equally if you see that your situation can never be the same again, you may want to organize a fall-back position, such as a job move, ahead of taking action

- If you do take action then it is best done promptly (or you may be asked, *Why ever didn't you say something at the time?*). Action must be directed at the right person – follow policy or pick carefully – and thereafter you need to be assertive and persistent to see the complaint through the various stages that are probably involved. It is easy to let the length and nature of the system put you off, yet you may feel you are acting for others as well as yourself

The legal implications here are beyond the scope of this short book, though it should be acknowledged that there are such implications (and if you experience such problems you may sensibly seek advice – and should do so early on – from a union or a staff association). It is also sensible to try to put yourself in other people's shoes. Asking, for instance, how someone you approach – perhaps in Personnel or Human Resources – will feel about such a thing and how they may react. The implications for an organization of some accusations in this sort of area are significant. Complaints can take up time and money and, at worst, create bad feeling or bad publicity on a wide front. Most organizations these days take such matters very seriously. If you ever get into a position where you have to take action about something of this sort, it may be worth remembering that:

- Organizations and the people in them can be held responsible both for the actions of others and their own policies and responses to such problems
- Just because there have been no other complaints does not mean there is no problem (in other words, you may not be the first to suffer; in which case, other evidence may appear as the process continues)
- Many employers are concerned to set an example, to set standards, and to have visible policies in place and be seen to react promptly and well

But organizations, however well they are set up to deal with such things, are also on the lookout for false claims; and in a litigious society there are some with motives such as revenge behind them. They also want to minimize the hassle caused by complaints. Recognizing this will help you to decide what to do and how to go about it.

At the risk of getting onto dangerous ground, it may be worth specifically mentioning discrimination against women here; I have made no point so far about how the differences between the sexes affects the topic under review. Indeed, there is a case that says it should make no difference. There can be problems, of course, and at least some of them, maternity leave for instance, are being dealt with increasingly successfully in most organizations. But there is a danger that such pronounced differences (and it may be the one man in an office full of women who is being discriminated against) begin to be blamed for every problem someone encounters. You are not promoted, put on the executive committee, or involved in a key project – because you are a woman. In which case it needs dealing with just as with any other form of discrimination. But maybe such problems are actually only an excuse, and it is always wise when there are problems to ask yourself if you are not a contributory factor in their occurrence.

As a man I must not underrate problems of this sort. However, many women I meet in organizations remind me of the quotation attributed to Charlotte Whitton: *Whatever women do, they must do twice as well as a man to be thought half as good. Luckily this is not difficult.*

❗ Always address such issues, always consider what you do carefully, always ● take formal advice, and do not allow yourself to feel isolated and alone.

Bear in mind too that the cause of the big problems may not always be other people; it might be you.

Creating Big Difficulties

There are some big problems that can arise from the action you take. So here, with no apology if they are obvious, are some real no-nos that can lead to potentially big and lasting problems, and which can sometimes be enough to destroy an otherwise good working relationship.

- Never bribe or blackmail your manager (with favors or threats of any sort)
- Never make important requests in a social setting (particularly not if the whole department has been in the pub for hours and the answer to almost anything would be yes)
- Never attempt to persuade them in difficult, perhaps contrived, circumstances (for example, without warning in a meeting when their manager is present too – floating an idea that you have primed them to approve, perhaps)
- Never exert emotional pressure (by bursting into tears, say)
- Never betray confidences willingly agreed
- Never criticize your boss behind their back (one thing you will never control is the grapevine – things said can come back to haunt you)
- Never lie to bolster a case (you reduce your chances of being believed in the future)

! ● Think before you take what seems like an easy fix. If it seems too easy, there is probably a catch – and the ramifications may not be predictable or desirable.

If All Else Fails

You should always bear human nature in mind. Many of the ideas that best deal with difficulties involve a soft approach. Saving face, bolstering confidence, making safe, and sheer tact all have a part to play. If you think diplomacy is another word for sledgehammer, then hold yourself in check; only rarely, and with great care, is a display of out-and-out – but nevertheless controlled – anger appropriate.

Beyond that, there is one other tactic that has not been mentioned: a little old-fashioned flattery (which, it is said, will get you anywhere).

Now care is clearly necessary here too; flattery is not something to direct at just anyone. But it could be appropriate. Just because you would see it as a ploy a million miles off, this does not mean that someone else, perhaps actually eager to be thought well of, would , not – and maybe your manager or other senior people with whom you deal are like this.

Note: if, when you read in the last paragraph: *just because you would see it as ...* , you said something to yourself like *Quite right, so I would* – then you have just proved to yourself how well flattery can work.

Success Breeds Success

The senior people you deal with are (in all probability!) not stupid. They are also, in part, personally motivated: they want things to go well, they want to minimize hassle, and they want a quiet life. Furthermore, they know a good thing when they see it. The ultimate trick to overcome difficulties and get lasting change is to *demonstrate* to them that the change works and that changes instigated by you are to be trusted. It should always be easier to achieve more of the same once they see the advantage of something.

For example, say that you succeed: something is – reluctantly – delegated and, surprise, surprise, all goes well, then the next time is – perhaps – viewed at least a little differently. As this process continues, a body of knowledge and experience is created and your boss will use this as a template against which to judge future suggestions. Some of this happens intentionally: a boss is watching to see how you do. Some of it happens subconsciously: as you talk about one thing a vision of something from the past flashes into their mind and this may encourage or discourage agreement depending upon how it went. On other occasions you can use this actively as you make suggestions – *Given how well X went, I wonder if Y* (which is recognizably similar in its implications) *could now be put into action?*

The use of clear examples in discussion, along with good preparation, should assist the process.

! Persuade them to try a change, show them that it is a change for the better **●** – and use it as evidence for more of the same.

The process of the past influencing the future is a core element of one particular regular event in most organizations: job appraisal meetings. In the next chapter we investigate how to get the most from them.

08

Getting the Most from Job Appraisals

> ❝ He who does not seek advice is a fool. His folly blinds him to Truth and makes him evil, stubborn, and a danger to his fellow men. ❞
>
> *Kahlil Gibran*

Love them or hate them, job appraisals are a part of most people's experience of employment and having a boss. They should be valuable events. They should be constructive and help make sure that in the period that follows them the likelihood of your working effectively is increased.

Despite the fact that they represent a real opportunity for the managers who conduct them, they are not universally well done. Both parties contribute and a bad manager may never be able to undertake a genuinely useful appraisal meeting. The person being appraised can help ensure it goes well too, so let us think about how you can get the best from yours. Though the focus here is on formal appraisal situations, evaluation takes many forms and some of the issues addressed in this chapter (for example, dealing with criticism) may be useful on other, less formal, occasions. Indeed, there should be many informal "appraisal moments" between a good boss and an employee throughout the year.

How Am I Doing?

Fact: how you progress in your job, the work you do, and the rewards you receive are, in every sense, largely down to how well you perform; and your manager is responsible for assessing that performance.

Most organizations have an appraisal process (some better than others) and there is only one way to view them – as an opportunity.

To get the best from them you need to:

* Know how your performance is viewed
* Review and learn from the past
* Seek improvements for the future
* Link the whole process to one of active career management and to the (increasing?) satisfaction and rewards you get – or want to get – from your job

To do this you need to *collaborate* with your manager to make your appraisal useful, and *influence* them to ensure the appraisal works for you. First, you need to have a clear understanding of what job appraisals are for and how they operate and are viewed in your organization (bearing in mind that your manager is almost certainly following a prescribed system – though this is no excuse for them being other than well done).

What Is The Purpose Of Appraisal?

Firstly, you need to understand why your organization has an appraisal process (apart from the not unimportant reason that good employment practice says it should. This fact can sometimes mean that appraisal is seen only as a necessary formality; if so, you should make it clear that *you want* it to be useful).

Reasons for appraisals, which should benefit both the individual and the organization, include:

- Reviewing individuals' past performance
- Planning their future work and role
- Setting specific individual future goals
- Agreeing and creating individual ownership of such goals
- Identifying development needs and setting up development and training activity
- On-the-spot coaching
- Obtaining feedback
- Reinforcing or extending the reporting relationship
- Acting as a catalyst to delegation
- Focusing on longer-term career progression
- Ensuring learning from experience
- Acting motivationally

Your appraisal review may focus on some or all of these; they are not mutually exclusive, but the relative emphasis on each may well vary. Overall, the intention, through all of the above, is to improve performance (taking the view that even good performance can often be improved), and make the likelihood of achieving future plans that much greater. An appraisal should not be a witch hunt and, although the past – and perhaps past mistakes – will be discussed, the main focus should always be on the future.

> **!** Understand what the organization
> regards as most important, and decide
> **●** what is most important to you.

How Appraisals Can Help You

To get the most from your appraisals, set yourself specific objectives under a number of headings:

- Planning how to make positive points about performance during the period under review
- Being ready to respond appropriately to points raised, including negative ones
- Projecting the right image
- Reviewing specific work plans for the next period ahead
- Reviewing factors upon which success in the future depends
- Identifying the need or desirability for training and development
- Looking ahead to longer-term career development
- Linking discussion to salary and benefits review

Your thinking about all of these needs to be positive. What needs to be done is not simply to think broadly about the sort of year it has been overall. It is to have clear intentions regarding not only what needs to (or will inevitably) be discussed, but about *what you can get from the discussion immediately* and in the future.

For example, in terms of training you might go to an appraisal with not only a training need identified, but also a recommendation as to what course you could attend as a result. Similarly, you might have specific areas of work that you would like to add to your portfolio. If so, go with some ideas of what might allow you to begin to do just that, and plan to describe why it would help the work as well as you.

! ● Appraisal, and all that goes with it, is about accelerating the process of learning from experience and maximizing its effectiveness.

Preparing For The Meeting

The first principle is that preparation does *not* start just before the meeting. If you are to discuss a whole year's activity (appraisal is often annual, though it may usefully be more frequent) you need to create and maintain a personal "appraisal file" so that you have all the necessary facts at your fingertips. Do not try to rely on your memory; to do so is simply not realistic.

The starting point for such a file is the documentation from your last appraisal (though obviously for a first one this is not possible). From then on you should make a point of collecting into this file copies of documents and notes you make that have a bearing on your next appraisal meeting. These will include:

- A note of any "significant events;" something about your first presentation, say, or the fact that you spoke at a trade association meeting or joined a significant committee

- Notifications of targets set, progress against them, and ultimate results achieved
- A note of any courses you have attended (as a minimum, file a copy of the course outline and a copy of any evaluation form you may have been asked to complete, perhaps together with a note of where any resumé notes issued on the course are to be found)
- Comments made to you by other people: maybe the M.D. wrote you a letter of congratulations, or a satisfied customer put pen to paper about a service you delivered
- A note – an explanation – about anything in the nature of mistakes linked to something about what it has taught you (see more of this below)

Other useful documents might be any memos, minutes of meetings, or other documents that may be useful as a record of your activity and outputs.

The idea is not to hoard everything, or spend a long time amassing this information; a note rather than a whole document may well be sufficient, and you simply need to spend an occasional moment throughout the year to ensure you create an appropriate and chronological record. You can sensibly match the information you gather to the topics that you know will feature in your forthcoming review. For example, if you are judged in part on your communications skills, then keeping some evidence of them in action may well help.

Remember that this is not solely a "boasting file"

containing references to your successes. If things do go wrong, or go less well than you had hoped, they may well be subject to review also – and this extends the information you can usefully collect. In this last category you are rarely simply mounting a defence – *It wasn't my fault* – but more often aiming to put yourself in a position to be able to demonstrate that you have learned and moved on from something that did cause a problem, and to make it clear there will be no repetition.

! **● The existence of such an "Appraisal file" makes preparation just before the event easier to do and more likely to make the appraisal effective.**

Now with good information to hand (and no need to rely on memory struggling to produce details from a year back) you can:

- Take the initiative where necessary
- Study the system (for example, making sure you are aware of the areas to be reviewed and are ready for them – see page 153)
- Ask for – with good notice – an agenda and details of what is planned to be discussed
- Prepare responses to specific points (including explaining why some things may not have gone well)
- Set yourself specific goals where appropriate (for example, *I will get agreement to attend a course on X in the next three months*)

Remember also to ask in good time if there are things you want added to the agenda, though expect to be asked why and have an answer ready.

**❗ In addition, always display a
constructive attitude to appraisal when
● you discuss it with your manager (and
especially when you ask for anything);
this too can help make things go well.**

There is important, useful, and possibly immediate action called for here – if you do not currently have an appraisal collection file, then start one today

What Will Be Discussed?

The formal appraisal system will alert you to the main topics that will be discussed. So, if this takes the form of standard processes or formats that will be used on the day, always have a good look through them. If it is your first appraisal in an organization or with a particular boss, then get any questions about the form and formalities of the process out of the way ahead of the meeting itself. You do not want to waste your allotted time by doing this on the day, and you need the information well ahead to assist your preparation.

The following are the sort of headings under which discussion will typically be organized.

Checklist: Appraisal Form
REVIEWING PAST PERFORMANCE

Agenda: the first questions may be linked to finalizing the agenda and arrangements for the meeting:

– What do you want to achieve in this meeting?

– Are there special areas you would like to spend time on? and why?

Job: here questions focus on the task in hand, both qualitatively with questions about what you like, have enjoyed, or found satisfying or challenging (or a problem); and *quantitatively* with questions about successes, and results and targets met or missed.

Relationships: investigating your work in terms of how it interacts with other people (whether peers, subordinates, or those elsewhere in the organization – or outside it – with whom you must work or liaise. Not least among these people are senior ones and your boss).

Development: *this heading allows a focus on skills*: what is needed for the job now, how you rate yourself at them, and whether there are skills that need adding or extending (or that are not currently being utilized)

Personal: an opportunity to think about things more in terms of feelings: have things been easy or difficult? Would you do things differently if it were possible? Are you being stretched, are you learning, or getting into a rut?

Special projects: some such heading allows specific, or more topical, areas of your work to be discussed

Make sure you anticipate (or ask about) as much as possible to be sure the intention is clear, and add (or ask for additions) for any other topics which the headings indicate *might* be omitted and which you want on the agenda. You may ask for additions that are not accepted, in which case you need to ask how and when these topics can be dealt with and agree a separate forum for them.

During The Meeting

A few key matters are of overriding importance here. You should consider:

- Your appearance (apart from being smartly turned out for an important occasion – your boss's boss may sit in – make sure you look well prepared and unflustered)
- Your manner (you should always be constructive, take your time, not be rushed, and give considered comments and responses)
- The procedure (your manager may have to abide by certain practices as much as you do; while a system is in force, respect it)
- Make notes. Listen, as in LISTEN! – and ask for a second or two to note things down if necessary
- Objectivity: appraisal is important for all concerned. It will not help if you lose your cool, and a calm, considered, and objective approach throughout is likely to be best

> **!** During any good appraisal meeting the appraisee – you – should do most of **● the talking; conducting yourself on this basis is good sense.**

Communication is not the easiest thing in the world, and misunderstandings are all too common. Remember the quotation attributed to the late American president Richard Nixon: *I know that you understand what you think I said, but I'm not sure you realize that what you heard is not what I meant.*

So be sure to keep things working well in such an important meeting (and any other, for that matter). Particularly:

- Ensure you are clear in what you say (planning helps here)
- Be descriptive (this is no place for saying – *Well, basically it was sort of difficult* – when what is necessary is a clear statement of the situation you faced over something)
- Concentrate on the *implications of things* and *the results* rather than the detail on the way through
- Offer proof of things if they may be contentious (and that means something *other* than you saying *I'm sure*); again, this may come back to preparation

Last but by no means least, never let anything go by that you are unclear about – if you are not sure what is being said, ask. This applies especially to things, and specific actions, relating to the future.

Follow-Up Action

Now, once the meeting is over, what do you do? Sigh with relief and pour yourself a stiff drink? Maybe, but actually several things need practical consideration:

- Take note of advice given (you might just have lessons to learn; indeed, a good boss should make sure you have)
- Allocate some time to review and take on board any personal consideration or action that is indicated
- Request written confirmation (this may be normal, but make sure you get not just a summary of the meeting, but also a specific note of all items and actions agreed – it might be best to take the initiative on some of this)
- Take any actions promised and remind your manager, if necessary, of action that they promised to take (perhaps to have another meeting to take some matter further, or to involve you in a specific project)
- Link your records of one meeting and your planning for the next similar session, even if this is a year ahead (in some organizations it may be more often) – appraisal is, or should be, a rolling process

 Use – and profit from – the outputs of your appraisal throughout the year.

If you are honest, then it is possible that one thing that will happen during your appraisal is that you will receive some criticism; indeed you may do so at other times as well. What should your reaction be to this?

Dealing With Criticism

Any appraisal is going to discuss difficulties – it goes with the territory – and you would be unusual (unbelievable?) if this never happens. This being the case, you must be ready to deal with this sort of comment.

Beyond a general desire to put the best complexion on everything, three intentions should be paramount:

- **Achieving accuracy**: here your intention is to ensure that the right facts are considered. Beware of the appraiser using vague statements like, *You're never on time with anything*, or *You never take on board the brief.* Such statements are unlikely to be true. But what *are* you late with, what do you tend to ignore, and what are the implications of this? It is easier to discuss specifics, and questions may well be the route to identify them. So, saying things like, *Can you give me an example?* will give you something more specific to discuss. The discussion can then more easily be kept factual and is more likely to prove useful.

  Never argue using anything other than the true facts, a to and fro argument about a general impression is unlikely to do anything but raise tempers. Checking what is really meant by a vague statement is the first step toward responding to what is said in the right way and making sure a discussion is constructive

- **Giving the impression of objectivity**: do
  not simply become defensive of criticism,
  or subsequent discussion is unlikely to be
  constructive. Using an acknowledgment to the
  criticism to position what follows is always useful.
  It:
  - Indicates you feel there is a point to discuss
    (if you do not, then we are back to achieving
    accuracy – see above)
  - Shows that you are not going to argue
    unconstructively
  - Makes it clear that you intend to respond in a
    serious and considered fashion
  - Gives you a moment to think (which may
    be very useful!) and sets up the subsequent
    discussion so that you can handle it better

Just a few words may be all that is necessary here.
Starting with a "yes" gives it power – *Yes, there was a problem
with that* – and sounds right even if your intention is to go
on to minimize the problem. Starting with a *No* distracts:
it is read as a denial, and the appraiser's mind becomes busy
planning a riposte

- Dealing with critical points raised: once a point is
  raised, clarified if necessary, and you accept that it
  needs addressing, then the job is to deal with the
  matter and do so in a way that progresses matters
  for the future. Mechanistically the options are few
  and therefore manageable. You may need to explain

why a difficulty occurred; if so, there are four routes to handling things:

1. **Remove the difficulty:** if possible, you can explain that what seemed like a difficulty or error was not. A delay, say, might not have been in an original plan, but caused no problem and made time so that something else was achieved as well.

2. **Reduce the difficulty:** maybe you have to acknowledge that there was some difficulty, but explain that it was of little significance.

3. **Turn the difficulty into a plus:** sometimes it is possible to argue that what might initially seem like a problem is actually not; in fact there may be a positive side. A delay might not have been in an original plan, but was included for a positive reason – there might only have been a real problem *without* the delay.

4. **Agree the difficulty:** after all, there is no point in trying to argue that black is white. Most ordinary mortals have some problems during a whole year of activity. Your job is not to persuade the appraiser that there were *no* problems, but to persuade the appraiser that, on balance, your year was a good one. Consider this carefully: nothing blights an appraisal more than a series of ill-fated fights over lost causes. They will just make you seem unreasonable and unwilling to focus on the positive.

Remember – the prime purpose of appraisal is to set the scene for successful work in the *coming* period, not to argue about what cannot be changed. No one can turn the clock back, but we can all learn from experience. So the key thing to include when the discussion touches on difficulties is the lessons that have been learned for the *future*.

The list of implications and actions to be taken here is considerable. For instance, failure may have come about:

- Because of unforeseen circumstances (and new procedures are necessary in case such circumstances occur again)
- Because you are starting to have to use skills not previously necessary in the job (and training may be needed to add them to your portfolio)
- Because you have made a simple slip (and only need to make a firm mental note not to allow it to recur)

There may be lessons to learn, but ultimately the emphasis needs to be on what happens next, and this allows a return to the most constructive elements of the dialog.

> **Dealing with criticism constructively allows negative matters to be put on one side and again allows you to take an initiative in managing your manager.**

Appraisals really do provide good, and regular, opportunities to work constructively with your boss and maximize the support that you get from them. This applies not only to the "annual appraisal," if that is what it is, but also to the whole process: the informal discussions that take place throughout the year, the thinking that is involved in planning for them, and the various actions that flow from it all.

If your past appraisals have left you upset or cold, and you feel you gained nothing from them – now is the time to start working to make the next one really useful for you and your boss.

Remuneration

No mention of salary has been made so far in this chapter because it is increasingly common for it to be considered separately from appraisal (something I agree is correct; it can skew the discussion and distract from the many other things an appraisal is about). But salary (and the benefits that go with it) is important and you want to be fairly rewarded. Appraisal is clearly linked to salary considerations, since in all likelihood you will be better rewarded if you are working effectively. In considering your own salary position:

- Be sure that you understand the system (usually there are grades and suchlike that keep salary matters well ordered)
- Do not make assumptions: for instance, people of the same age and experience may not be paid the same, even when they are doing comparable jobs, and for good reasons
- Do not take the grapevine as gospel. If there is one area where the truth is rarely told, it is when salaries are discussed amongst colleagues

- Remember that there is more than salary involved, and consider the whole rewards package
- Balance factors such as risk, salary, and job satisfaction; realistically, most jobs are to some degree a compromise
- Link appraisal and salary request/negotiations by all means; there is nothing better to base a request on than your performance

Keep money in perspective. To quote Harry Raelbrook (of Rael Brook shirt fame): I give this tip to any youngster who wants to be a success.

I advise him that if he wants to make money, he must never think about money. If you are continually thinking in terms of cash, you just will not take the necessary calculated risks. It is a fair point. Money results, or can do, from the success of what you do and how you do it. Never forget your financial objectives, but never view them in isolation either.

Ultimately, job satisfaction comes from doing a job you like (and that includes it being a challenge or having whatever other desirable characteristics you put on it – including a good boss and a constructive relationship with them) and being appropriately rewarded for doing it. The Business Solutions series covers a variety of aspects concerned with making your working time successful; here the focus is on one specific factor – working with your boss.

The quality of this relationship can dilute your job satisfaction and success, or act positively to enhance it, sometimes in a major way.

Perhaps remuneration is a good point on which to end. Ultimately, a good relationship, especially with a good boss, helps you to do a good job, and being rewarded effectively should follow. But, as this book makes clear, success is in the detail. To help you draw up an action plan, the last section summarises some key issues.

Afterword

> ❝ Wisdom is not the exclusive possession of management. ❞
> *Akio Morita (When Ceo Of Sony)*

Key Issues

Overall, managing the necessary working relationship with your boss, or anyone else senior with whom you liaise or collaborate, is something that takes place largely *through* other things that are going on rather than primarily being an activity in its own right.

For example, in communications, projects, and meetings you may need not only to do these things, but also to add an element of activity into the process that manages relationships as well as the circumstance.

By and large, everything that you want to achieve to have a good relationship with your boss is going to help you do your job better – and that is what your boss wants too, so there is no inherent clash. Some managers can undeniably be difficult, cussed sometimes, but many problems are more to do with circumstances (classically with lack of time) than to radically opposed views.

Overall, it may help to view the process as one that is ongoing and *educational*. You are helping them to do the right things rather than seeing it as any kind of adversarial process.

As with so much else in business and organizations there are few magic formulae (if any) and success is in the detail. What matters here is things and approaches that will help you be effective. There is no better way of getting on with your boss than being effective, and practices which indicate that this is likely and that you are a force to be reckoned with rather than a mere minion, help make the process work well. The following list is typical of the kinds of things you can do. In part it recaps, and it is no doubt incomplete and can be added to. What you need to do is decide upon the specific approaches that are most likely to help you in the situation in which you work: adopting, adapting, or adding ideas and methodology to produce a mix that works for you. For example:

- **Make yourself indispensable:** especially by doing what other people do poorly or dislike and avoid (this refers to meaningful tasks; do not characterize yourself as the departmental skivvy)
- **Make your boss look good:** do some public relations for them and the department; it will be appreciated and they may feel they owe you a favor
- **Go the extra mile:** do more than you are asked and always be willing to help in a crisis
- **Keep your ear to the ground and be a useful source of information:** this can begin to work in the reverse direction: your boss asks you what you know about something or starts to regard, and

describe you as, an expert on something

- **Work effectively when you are not supervised:** if the boss is away or just leaving you alone for a while, make sure that things go well, deadlines are met, and nothing creates problems for their return

- **Reflect your boss's goals:** your work should complement, and extend, their own

- **Note extensions to your work:** when you go further than your job description, make a note; if things take you into new and desirable areas then they may be topics worth discussing at your next appraisal. Job descriptions should not be written in tablets of stone; they can be amended and your job can grow with them. Equally, do not refuse or kick up a fuss about anything that has the temerity to go over the edge of your prescribed list of responsibilities; some flexibility is appreciated

- **Volunteer:** for things that either your boss or others are seeking to allocate, but do so carefully – there are what I call "black-hole jobs" that are simply guaranteed to cause you grief. For example, volunteer to organize the firm's annual Christmas party and, however you do it, you will never please everyone

- **Be a team player:** that means both playing your part and working well with others and, if necessary, encouraging them to do the same

- **Avoid office politics:** well, by all means keep your ear to the ground and tap in to the office grapevine

– but it is dangerous to be seen as the originator or propagator of rumours, especially if they prove unfounded

- **Be honest:** white lies are sometimes acceptable; otherwise there are no grades of honesty – you can find yourself honest or fired

- **Be a good collaborator:** your work may involve you with many other people in ways that are easy or anything but easy (you may also like them or not), but it is sensible to make the best of it and useful to be known as one who does so

- **Match your way of working to job and career:** you have to keep an eye on what you need to do to be effective in your current job and link to your private career plan too (see the book *Detox Your Career*). Sometimes objectives will clash and you need to watch the balance carefully

- **Be positive:** even when dealing with problems, the best approach is usually one of optimism; doomsayers are not usually appreciated and you rarely get any thanks or kudos for saying, *I told you so*

- **Watch the big picture:** this is a prime characteristic of senior people; do not get swamped by and lost in details to the exclusion of all else

- **Watch what works and who succeeds in your organization:** and learn from it

- **Develop your skills:** always push for the training you think you deserve and which will be useful, even if it is difficult to get; the new or improved

skills you ultimately acquire will be appreciated
and make you better able to take on new things

- **Be generous to others:** sharing knowledge and
  passing on skills will do you more good than the
  reverse, even though this may seem to produce
  some momentary advantage to others
- **Look the part:** corporate culture affects what this
  means; always look efficient
- **Deliver:** hit deadlines, keep promises, and do what
  you say you will do
- **Make suggestions:** especially those that positively
  affect costs, profits, or improve operations in some
  way (and do not expect them all to be taken up)
- **Break bad news sooner rather than later:** if
  you have to tell the boss something that makes
  for difficulties, do not compound the problem
  by delay, which may just make a resolution more
  difficult
- **Keep any information you use (or supply to
  others) up to date:** any shortfall here can quickly
  make you look inefficient
- **Ask for feedback:** from anyone and everyone
  whose opinion might help you, and do not reject it
  out of hand if it is not what you want
- **Be courteous where appropriate:** if things are
  done which do help you, thank people and do so
  sincerely
- **Do not make enemies:** it may be unavoidable
  occasionally, but remember that you never know

when a good relationship with someone may be useful in the future; if you burn your bridges in unthinking temper you may rue the day later

- **Take initiatives:** if you never stick your neck out you remove the possibility of chances to shine
- **Be enthusiastic:** if you want to push a line, a plan, or persuade someone about an idea, you must have the courage of your convictions. If you clearly believe it is important, it is easier to persuade others to share your view; enthusiasm is infectious
- **Be responsible:** for everything you do (including occasionally what you do that is wrong)

All the above, and more no doubt, have a real practical edge. If all your efforts to succeed are seen as toadying or as attempts simply to curry favor, and thus as being for your own purposes rather than to help overall departmental or corporate success, then they are apt to backfire. Seek what you want through the way you work successfully as your boss wants, and they will see you as an asset, one worth cultivating

Looking To The Future

At the end of the day, managing your boss can be a full-time job! It must be done in parallel with the job of doing your job, and getting the results you want (and that your boss wants). It requires a range of skills, particularly in various forms of communication. It also demands patience, persistence, and assertiveness; and it needs some real care and consideration.

Your objectives here are essentially twofold (and they overlap):

- Ensure you can do your job effectively – with excellence – and achieve, or exceed, your targets
- Enhance your job satisfaction and the career progress you want to make towards new challenges

Having a good boss is something that is created as much by you as it is simply a fact of life. And, make no mistake, a good boss is probably the most positively influential resource anyone can have. It may seem superficially attractive to have a boss who keeps out of the way, does not interfere, and whom you can run rings around. Not so. Having a boss that challenges you, involves you, trusts you, and supports you is going to get you very much further in your job and career.

Such a boss can be annoying, difficult, and is unlikely to make for a quiet life. But I have had bosses good and bad and I know not only which I preferred, but also which helped me to progress and enjoy what I did the most.

Getting the relationship with your boss right can make the difference between having just a job or having a career that rewards and satisfies; and, of course, the right relationship can ultimately benefit your boss too, improving both how they feel about their job and what they can achieve overall. The process of creating a good relationship is not always easy, though it repays the effort it takes. So, finally, remember the old saying:

66 Always do exactly what your boss would do – if, that is, they knew what they were talking about! **99**

About the Author

Patrick Forsyth has himself had a successful career; or certainly he likes to think so. He now runs his own company, Touchstone Training & Consultancy, specializing in the improvement of marketing, sales, and communications skills, and says he has now "found an employer I can really get on with."

He began his career in publishing and worked happily in sales, in promotion and marketing there, before escaping to something better paid just ahead of terminal poverty. He then worked for the Institute of Marketing (now the Chartered Institute), first in research, latterly in the promotion of their training products and publications. He helped set up an export assistance scheme and then moved into consultancy, first in a management marketing position. Much against his better judgment initially, he was soon persuaded to get involved in client work and began to undertake consulting assignments and conduct training courses.

His work also began to take on an international

dimension. He helped set up offices in Brussels and Singapore and began to work and lecture overseas. He still travels regularly, especially to South East Asia, and has, over the years, worked in most countries in continental Europe, including the former Eastern Bloc. Other, more occasional, destinations have included America, Australia, East Africa, Argentina, and Borneo.

After some years at director level in a medium-sized marketing consultancy, he set up his own organization in 1990. He conducts training for organizations in a wide range of industries, and has conducted public courses for such bodies as the Institute of Management, the City University Business School, and the London Chamber of Commerce and Industry.

In addition, he writes on matters of management and marketing in a variety of business journals, and is the author of more than 50 business books, corporate publications and training material.

Books in the Business Solutions Series

EFFECTIVE DECISION MAKING
10 steps to better decision making and problem solving | Jeremy Kourdi

BRILLIANT COMMUNICATION
5 steps to communicating your message clearly and effectively | Patrick Forsyth

THE NEW RULES OF ENTREPRENEURSHIP
What it really takes to become a savvy and successful entrepreneur | Rob Yeung

GREAT SELLING SKILLS
How to sell anything to anyone | Bob Etherington

THE NEW RULES OF JOBHUNTING
A modern guide to finding the job you want | Rob Yeung

MANAGE YOUR BOSS
How to create the ideal working relationship | Patrick Forsyth

GREAT NEGOTIATING SKILLS
The essential guide to getting what you want | Bob Etherington

SURVIVING OFFICE POLITICS
Coping and succeeding in the workplace jungle | Patrick Forsyth

ESSENTIAL TIME MANAGEMENT
How to become more productive and effective | Brett Hilder

SIMPLY A GREAT MANAGER
The fundamentals of being a successful manager | Mike Hoyle & Peter Newman